W9-BCG-514

GRAPHIC HISTORY

THE CURSE OF KING TUT'S TOMB

by Michael Burgan
illustrated by Barbara Schulz

Consultant:
Carolyn Graves Brown
Curator, Egypt Centre, University of Wales Swansea
Swansea, Wales

Capstone press

Mankato, Minnesota

Graphic Library is published by Capstone Press,
151 Good Counsel Drive, P.O. Box 669, Mankato, Minnesota 56002.
www.capstonepress.com

Printed in the United States of America

1 2 3 4 5 6 10 09 08 07 06 05

Library of Congress Cataloging-in-Publication Data
Burgan, Michael.
The curse of King Tut's tomb / by Michael Burgan; illustrated by Barbara Schulz.
p. cm.—(Graphic library. Graphic history)
Includes bibliographical references and index.
ISBN 0-7368-3833-3 (hardcover)
ISBN 0-7368-5244-1 (paperback)
1. Tutankhamen, King of Egypt—Tomb—Juvenile literature. 2. Blessing and cursing—Egypt—Juvenile literature. I. Barbara Schulz, ill. II. Title. III. Series.
DT87.5.B83 2005
932'.014—dc22 2004020452

Summary: Follows the discovery and excavation of King Tutankhamen's tomb and the myth of the curse that afflicted those involved in the tomb's exploration.

Editor's note: Direct quotations from primary sources are indicated by a yellow background.

Direct quotations appear on the following pages:

Pages 9, 11, 14, from *The Tomb of Tut.ankh.Amen, Discovered by the Late Earl of Carnarvon and Howard Carter* by Howard Carter and A. C. Mace (London: Cassell and Company, Ltd., 1923).

Page 21, from "Effects of Digestive Disfunction" by Dr. Skye Weintraub (http://www.femcentre.com/digestive1.pdf).

Page 22, from *The Complete Tutankhamun: The King, the Tomb, the Royal Treasure* by Nicholas Reeves (New York: Thames and Hudson, 1990).

Art Directors
Jason Knudson
Heather Kindseth

Storyboard Artists
Sandra D'Antonio
Jason Knudson

Colorist
Ben Hunzeker

Editor
Amanda Doering

Acknowledgment
Capstone Press thanks Philip Charles Crawford, Library Director, Essex High School, Essex, Vermont, and columnist for *Knowledge Quest*, for his assistance in the preparation of this book.

TABLE OF CONTENTS

CHAPTER 1

THE MUMMY'S CURSE IS BORN

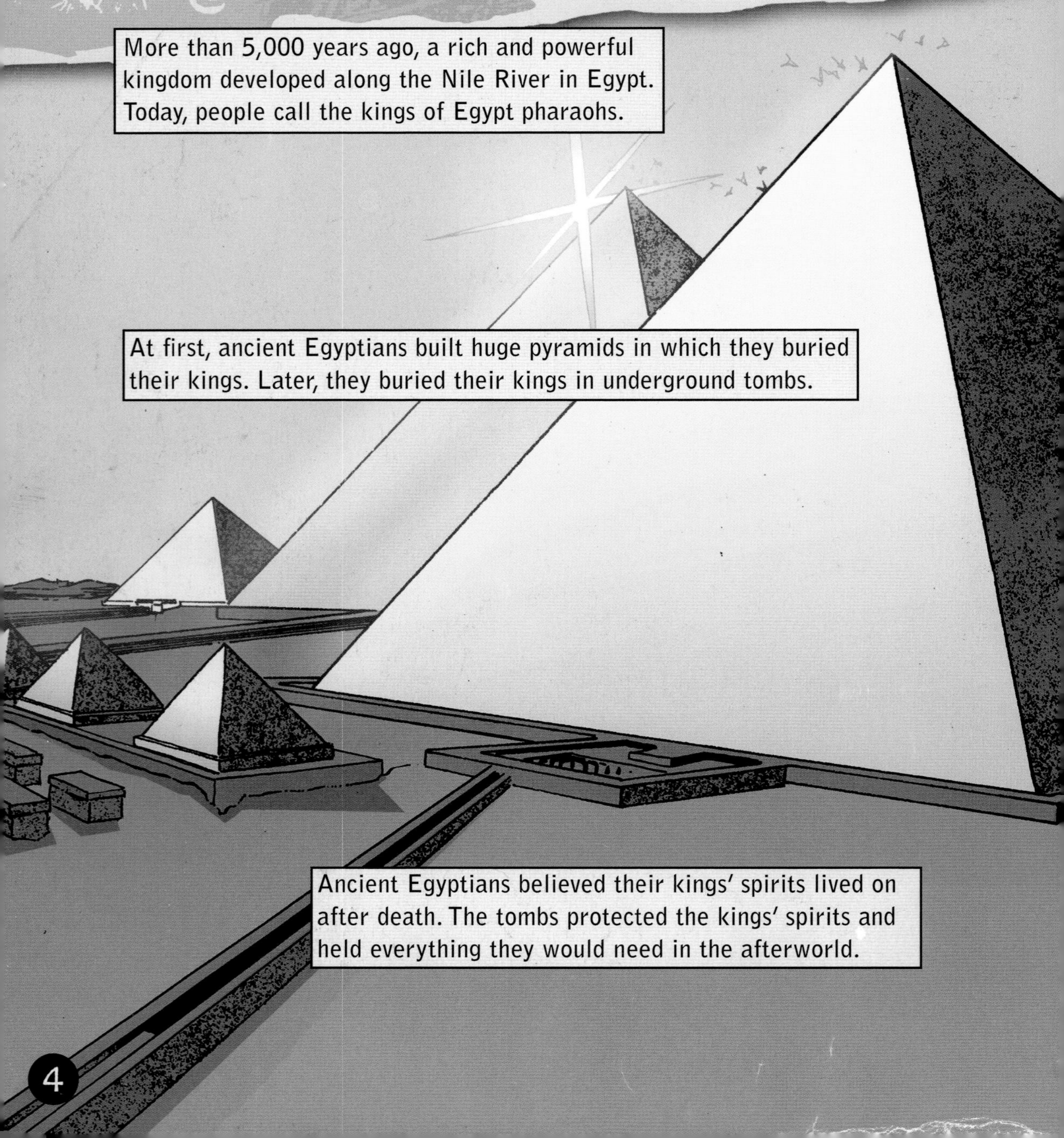
More than 5,000 years ago, a rich and powerful kingdom developed along the Nile River in Egypt. Today, people call the kings of Egypt pharaohs.
At first, ancient Egyptians built huge pyramids in which they buried their kings. Later, they buried their kings in underground tombs.
Ancient Egyptians believed their kings' spirits lived on after death. The tombs protected the kings' spirits and held everything they would need in the afterworld.

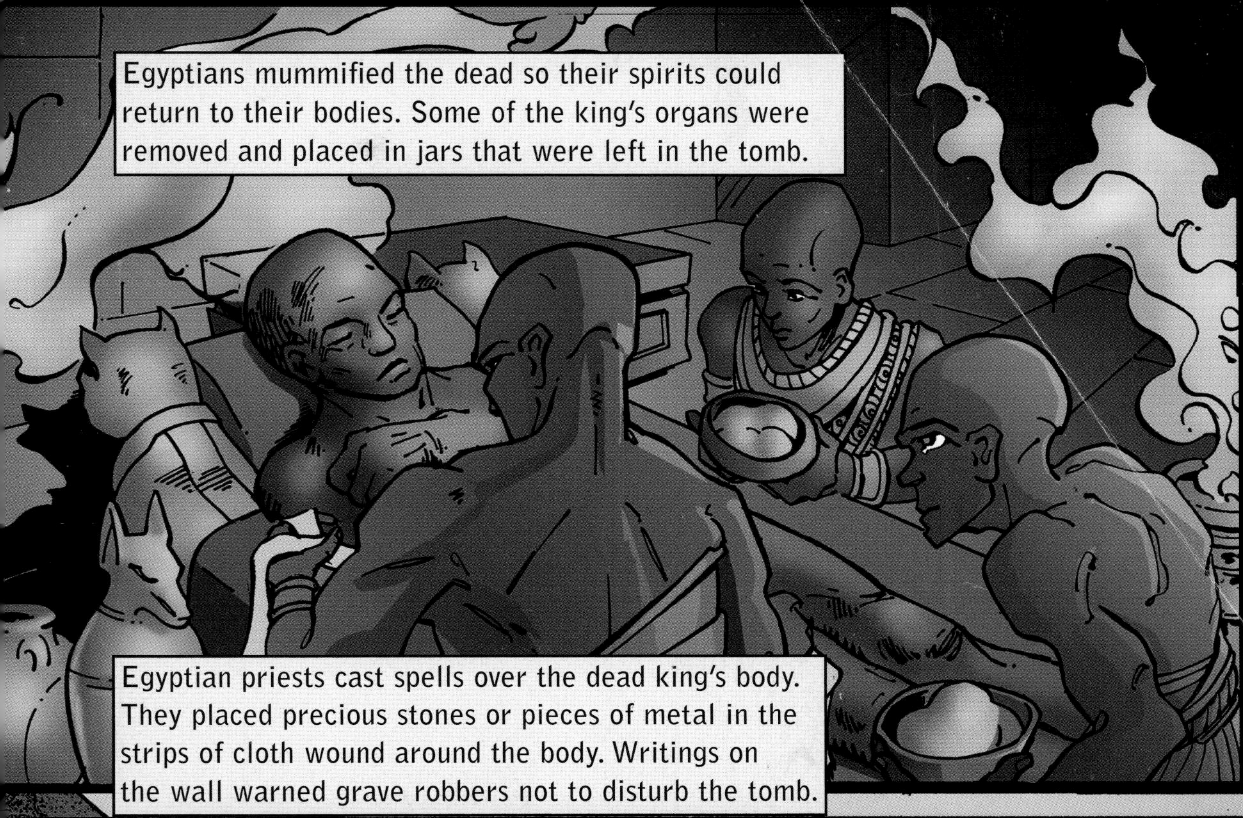
Egyptians mummified the dead so their spirits could return to their bodies. Some of the king's organs were removed and placed in jars that were left in the tomb.
Egyptian priests cast spells over the dead king's body. They placed precious stones or pieces of metal in the strips of cloth wound around the body. Writings on the wall warned grave robbers not to disturb the tomb.

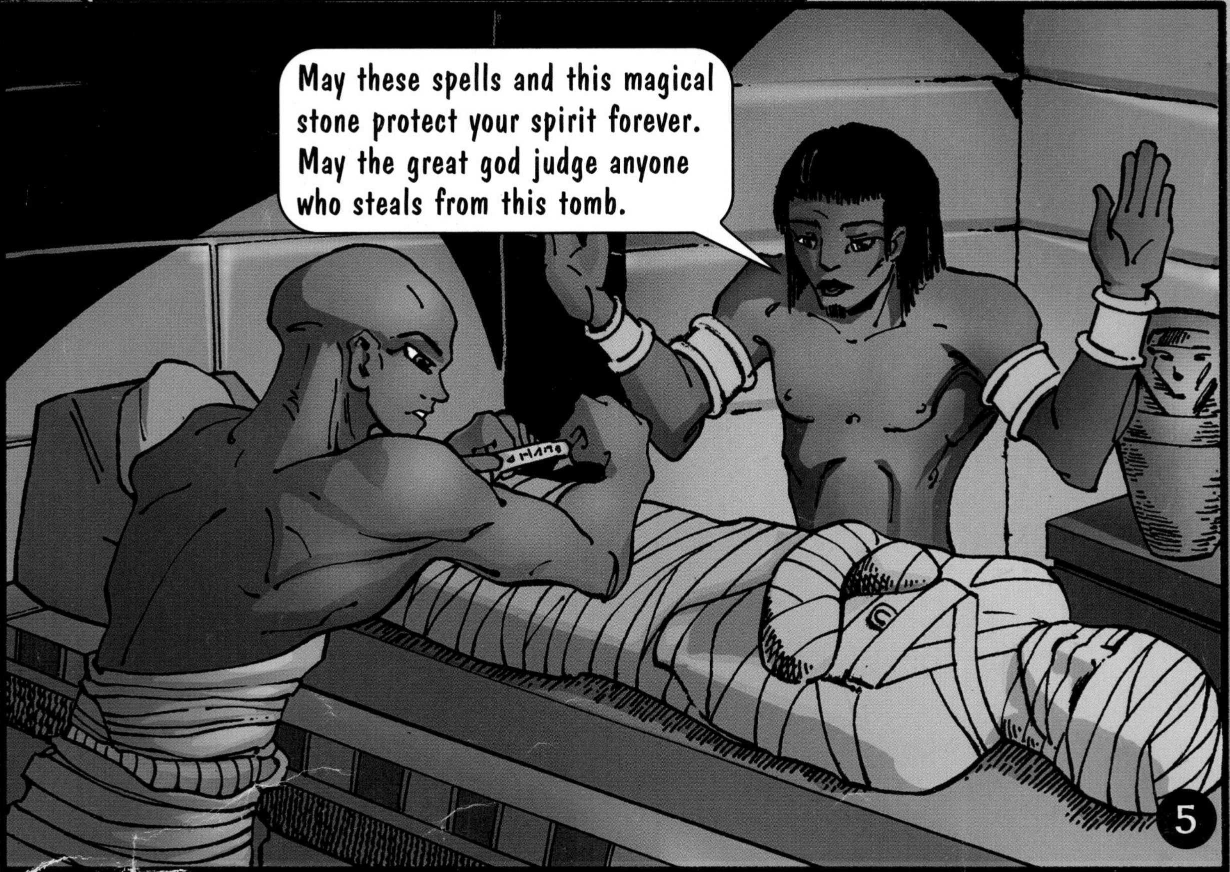
May these spells and this magical stone protect your spirit forever. May the great god judge anyone who steals from this tomb.

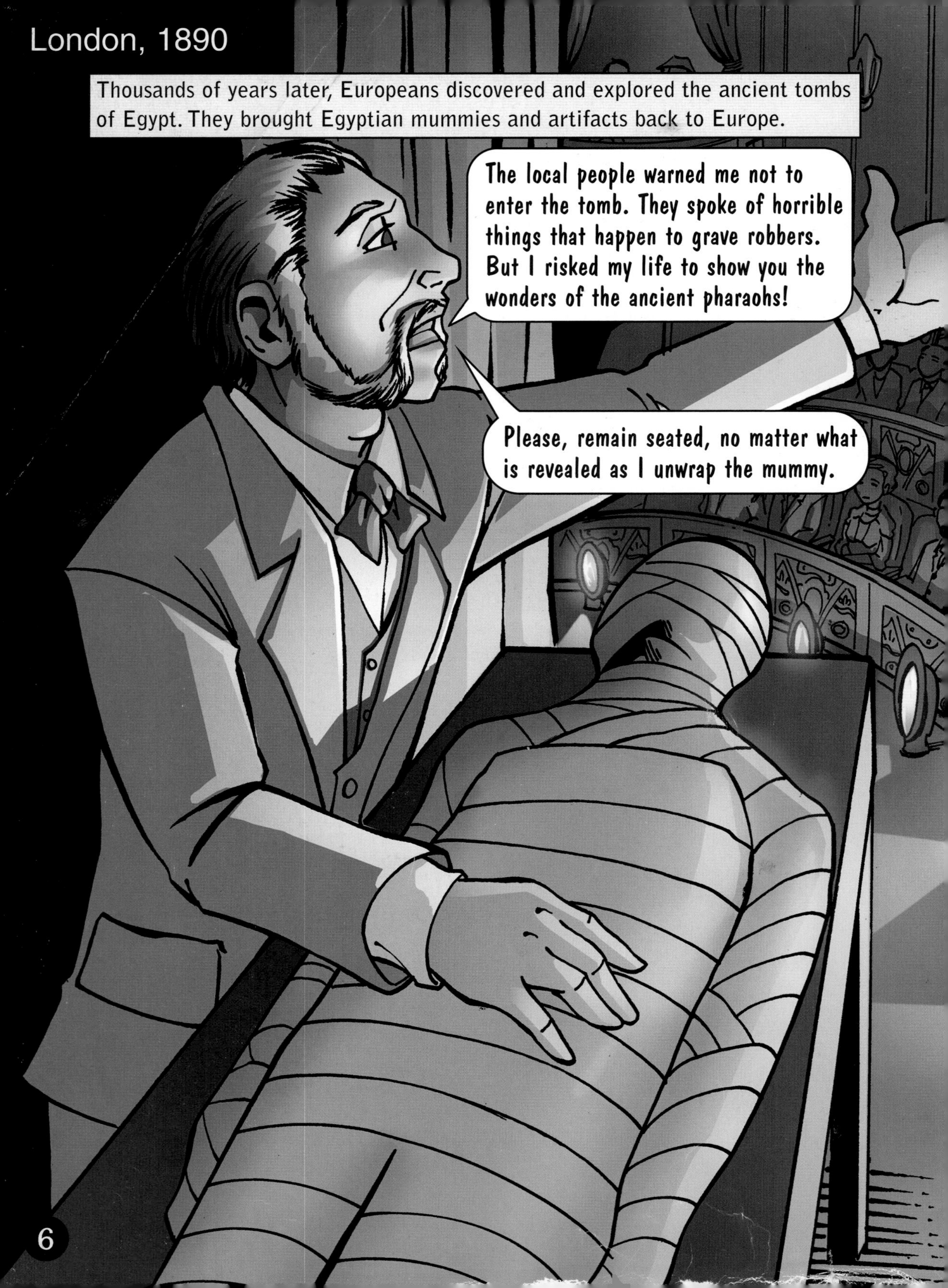
London, 1890
Thousands of years later, Europeans discovered and explored the ancient tombs of Egypt. They brought Egyptian mummies and artifacts back to Europe.
The local people warned me not to enter the tomb. They spoke of horrible things that happen to grave robbers. But I risked my life to show you the wonders of the ancient pharaohs!
Please, remain seated, no matter what is revealed as I unwrap the mummy.

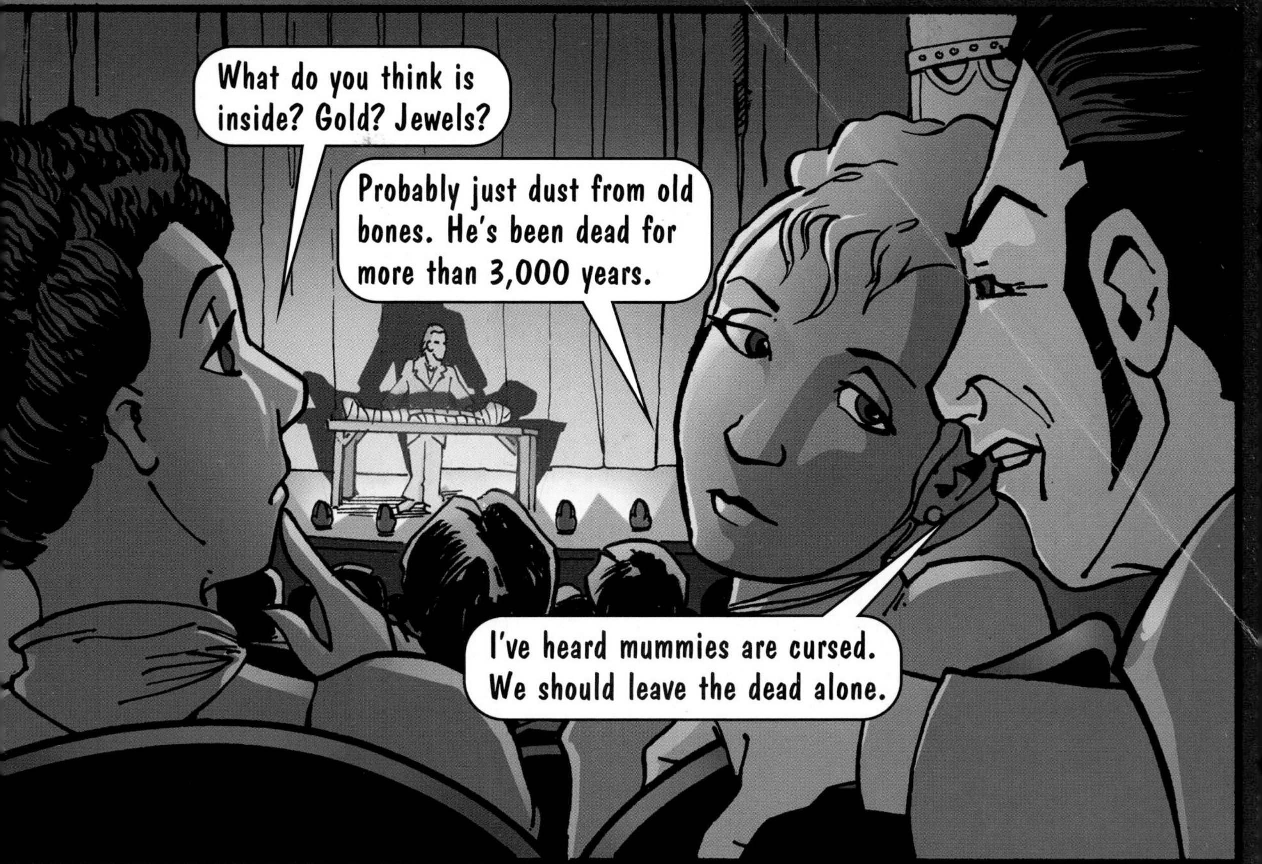
What do you think is inside? Gold? Jewels?
Probably just dust from old bones. He's been dead for more than 3,000 years.
I've heard mummies are cursed. We should leave the dead alone.

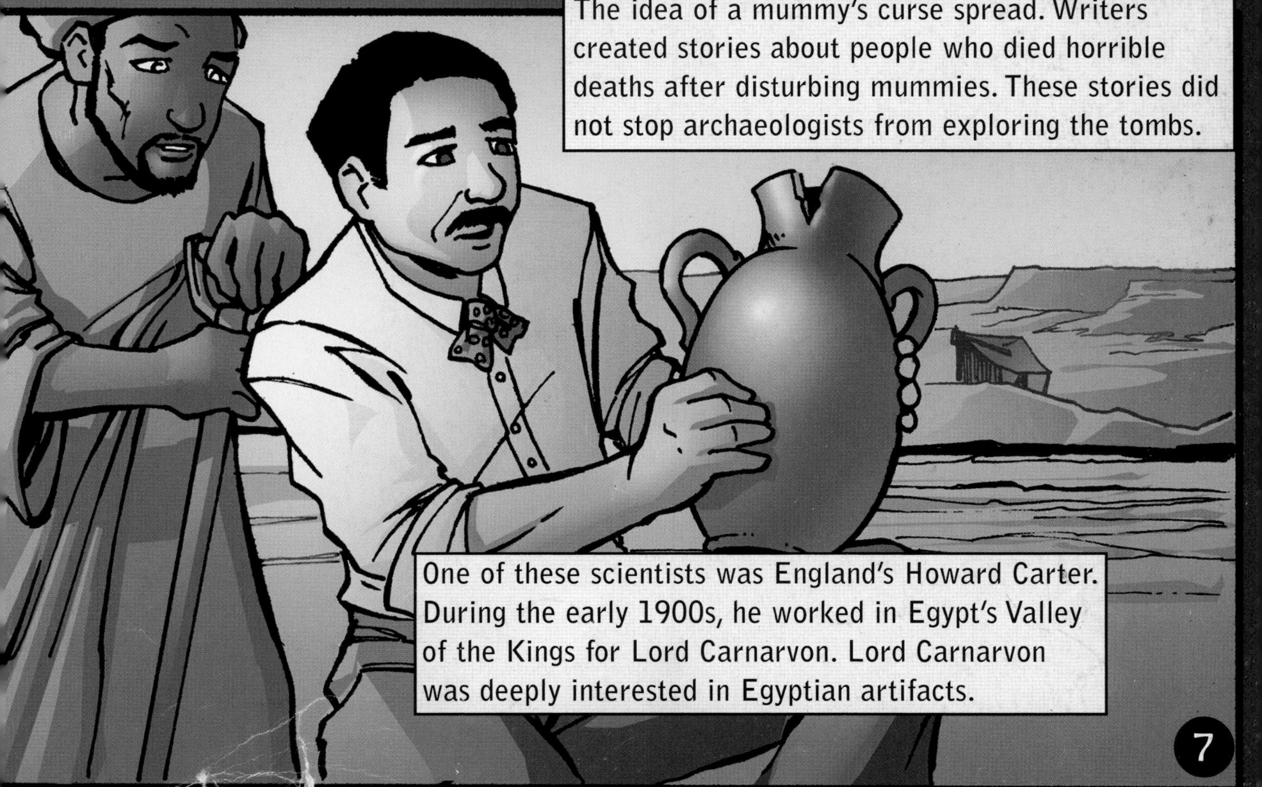
The idea of a mummy's curse spread. Writers created stories about people who died horrible deaths after disturbing mummies. These stories did not stop archaeologists from exploring the tombs.
One of these scientists was England's Howard Carter. During the early 1900s, he worked in Egypt's Valley of the Kings for Lord Carnarvon. Lord Carnarvon was deeply interested in Egyptian artifacts.

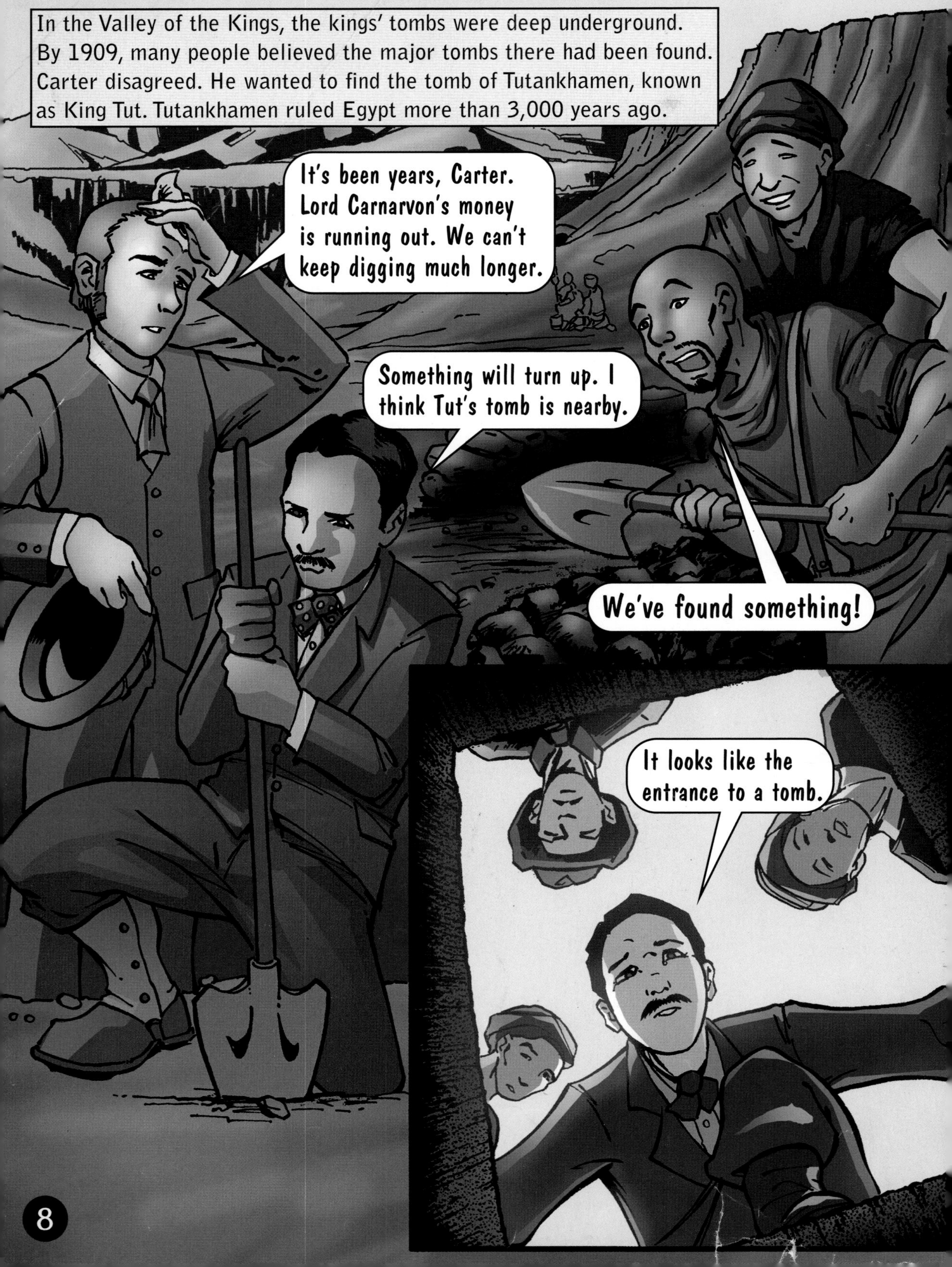
In the Valley of the Kings, the kings' tombs were deep underground. By 1909, many people believed the major tombs there had been found. Carter disagreed. He wanted to find the tomb of Tutankhamen, known as King Tut. Tutankhamen ruled Egypt more than 3,000 years ago.
It's been years, Carter. Lord Carnarvon's money is running out. We can't keep digging much longer.
Something will turn up. I think Tut's tomb is nearby.
We've found something!
It looks like the entrance to a tomb.

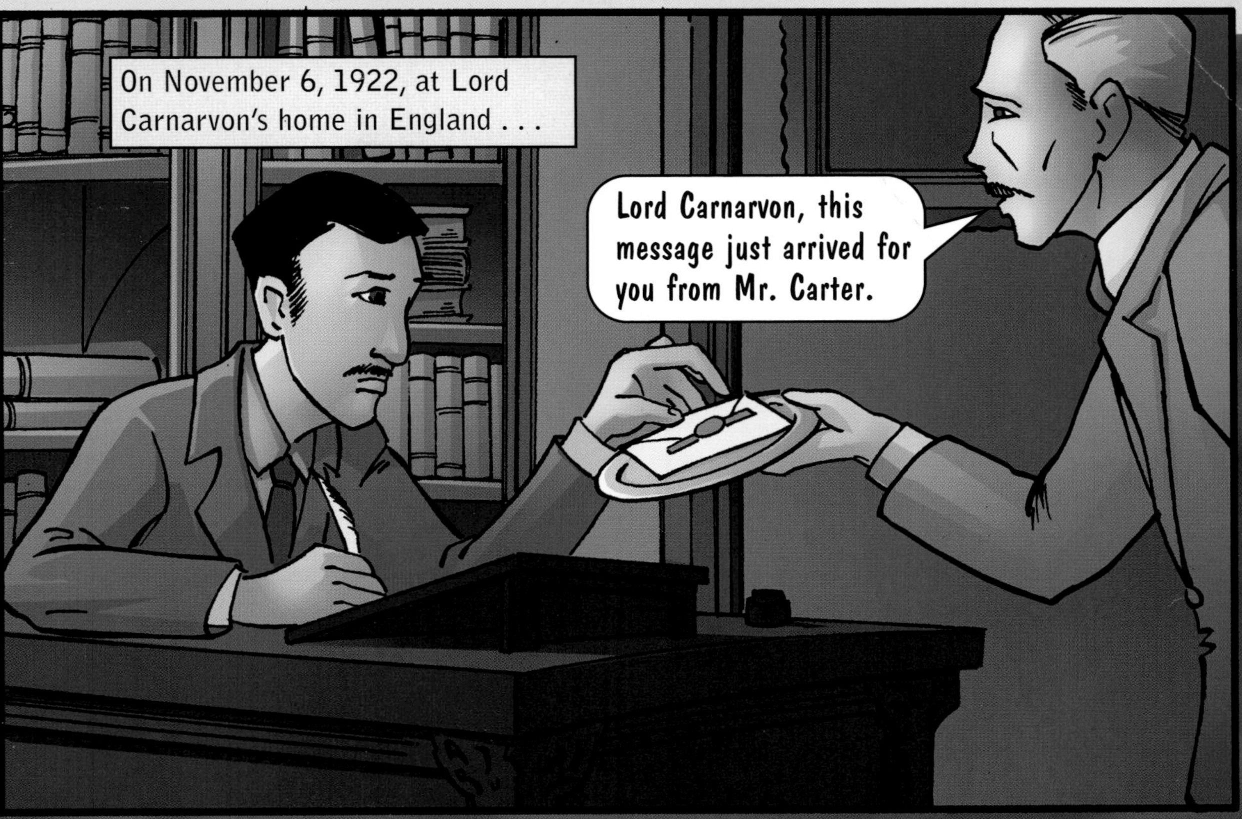
On November 6, 1922, at Lord Carnarvon's home in England . . .
Lord Carnarvon, this message just arrived for you from Mr. Carter.

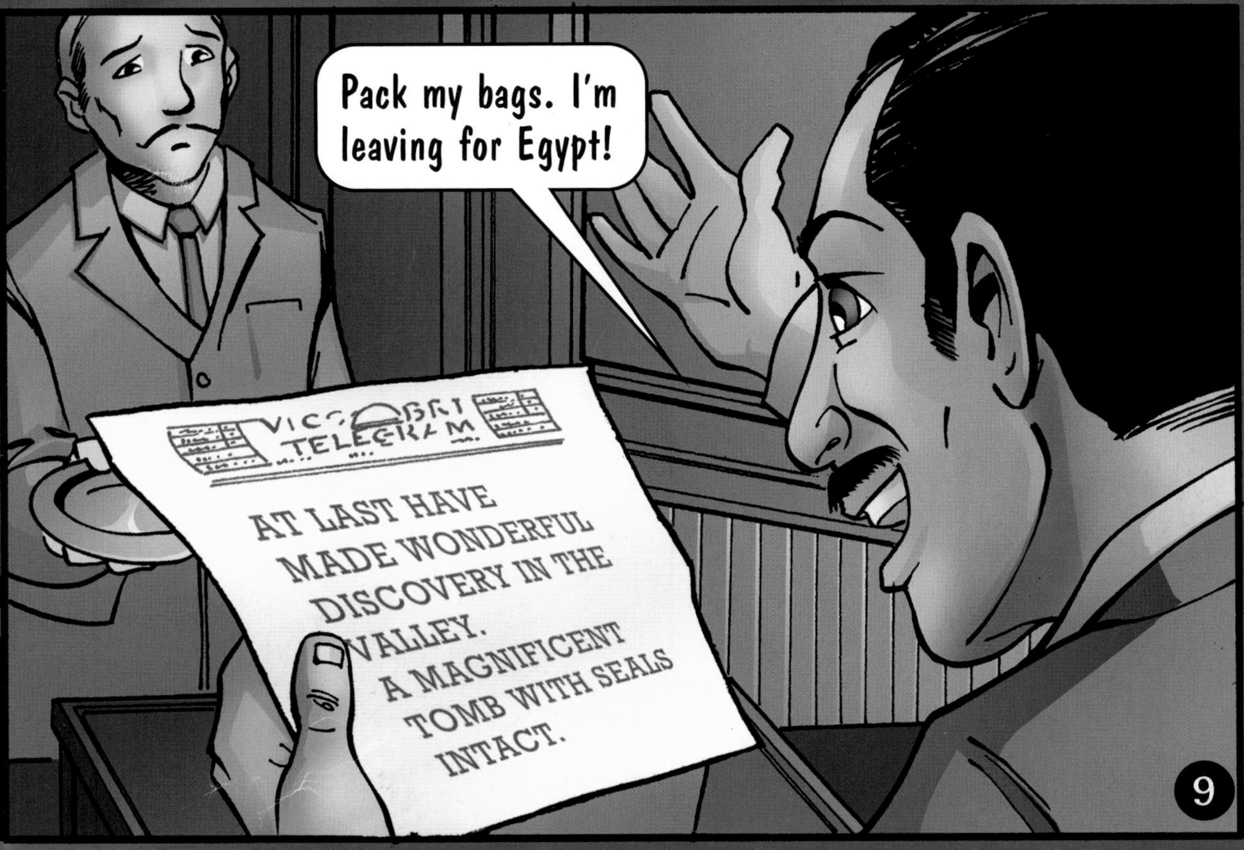
Pack my bags. I'm leaving for Egypt!
AT LAST HAVE MADE WONDERFUL DISCOVERY IN THE VALLEY. A MAGNIFICENT TOMB WITH SEALS INTACT.

Chapter 2

An Amazing Discovery

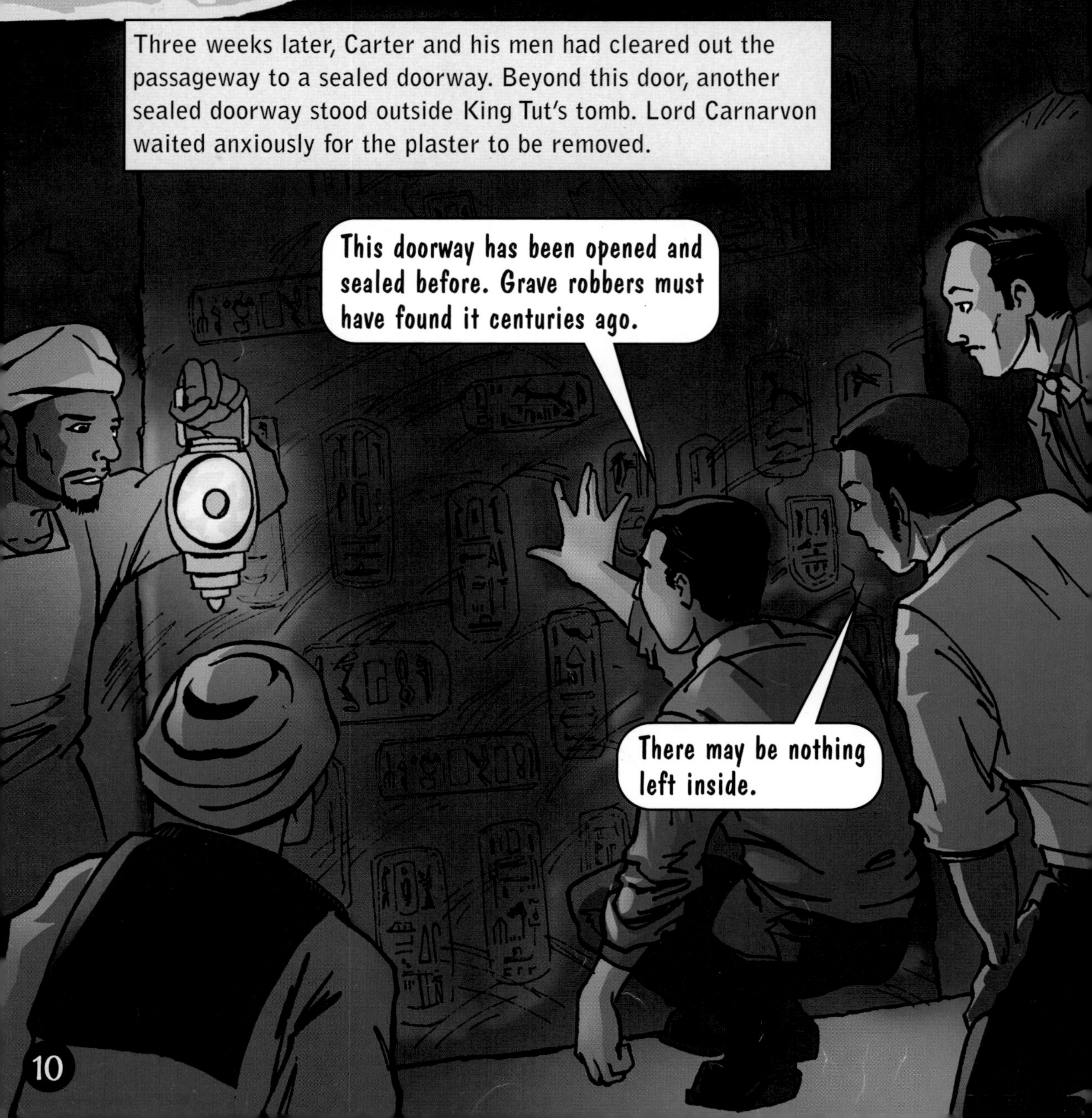

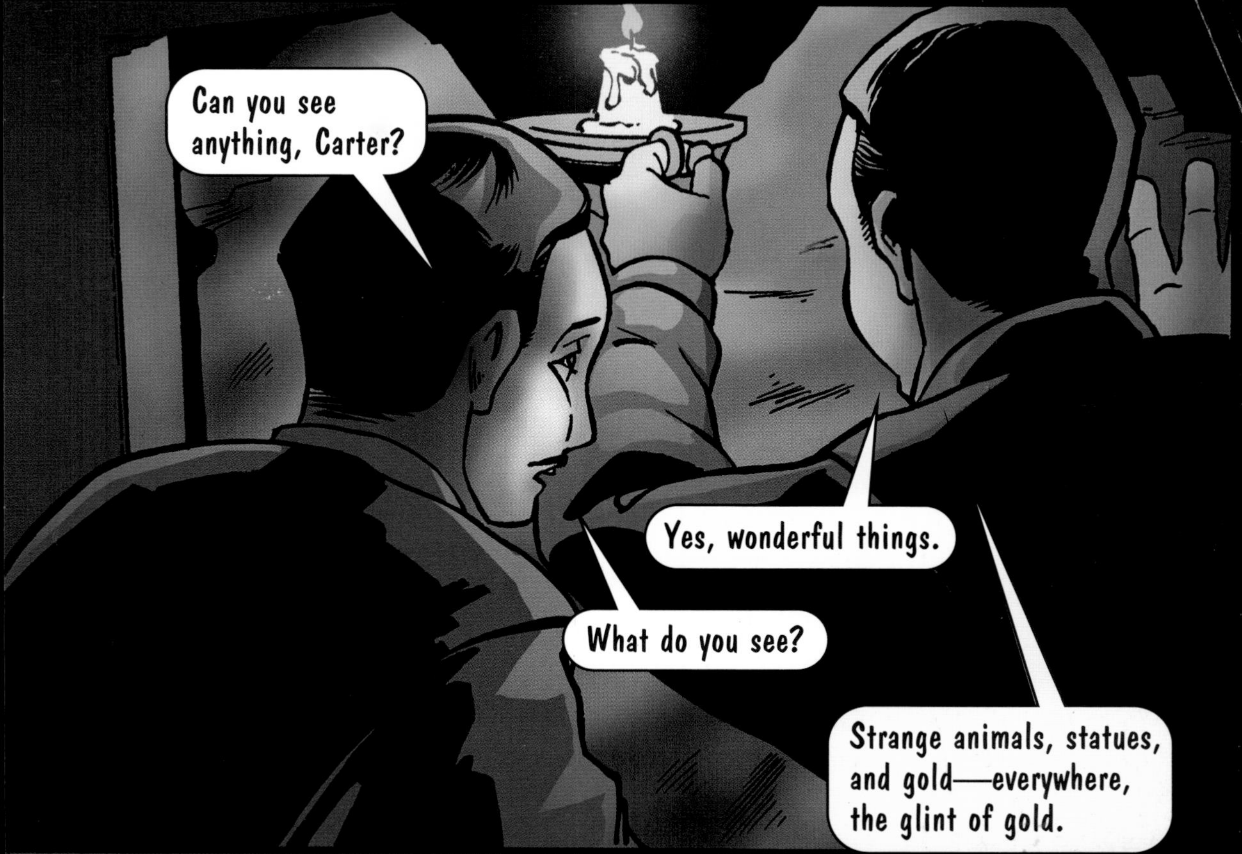
Can you see anything, Carter?
Yes, wonderful things.
What do you see?
Strange animals, statues, and gold—everywhere, the glint of gold.

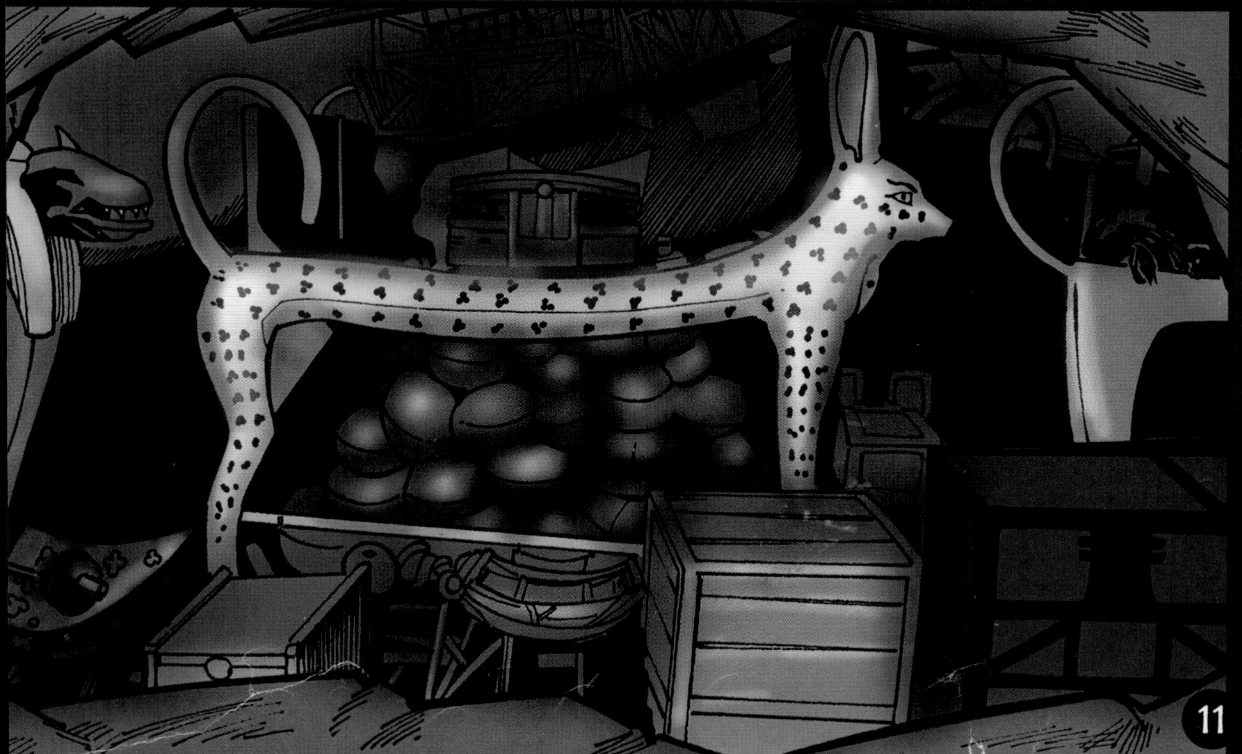

Carter and his crew began exploring the tomb and its treasures. They numbered each item they found. It would take Carter years to examine everything in the tomb's many rooms.

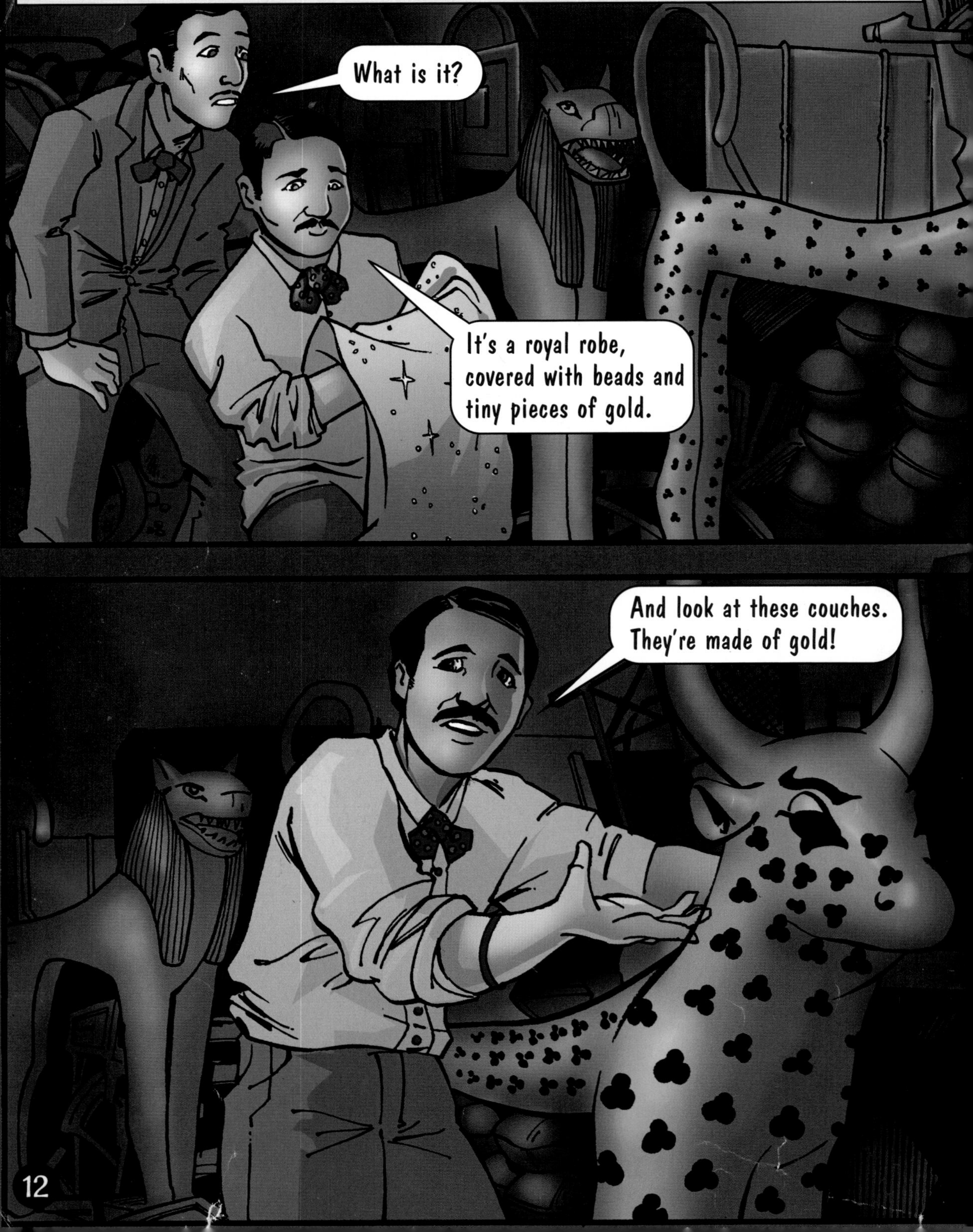
What is it?
It's a royal robe, covered with beads and tiny pieces of gold.
And look at these couches. They're made of gold!

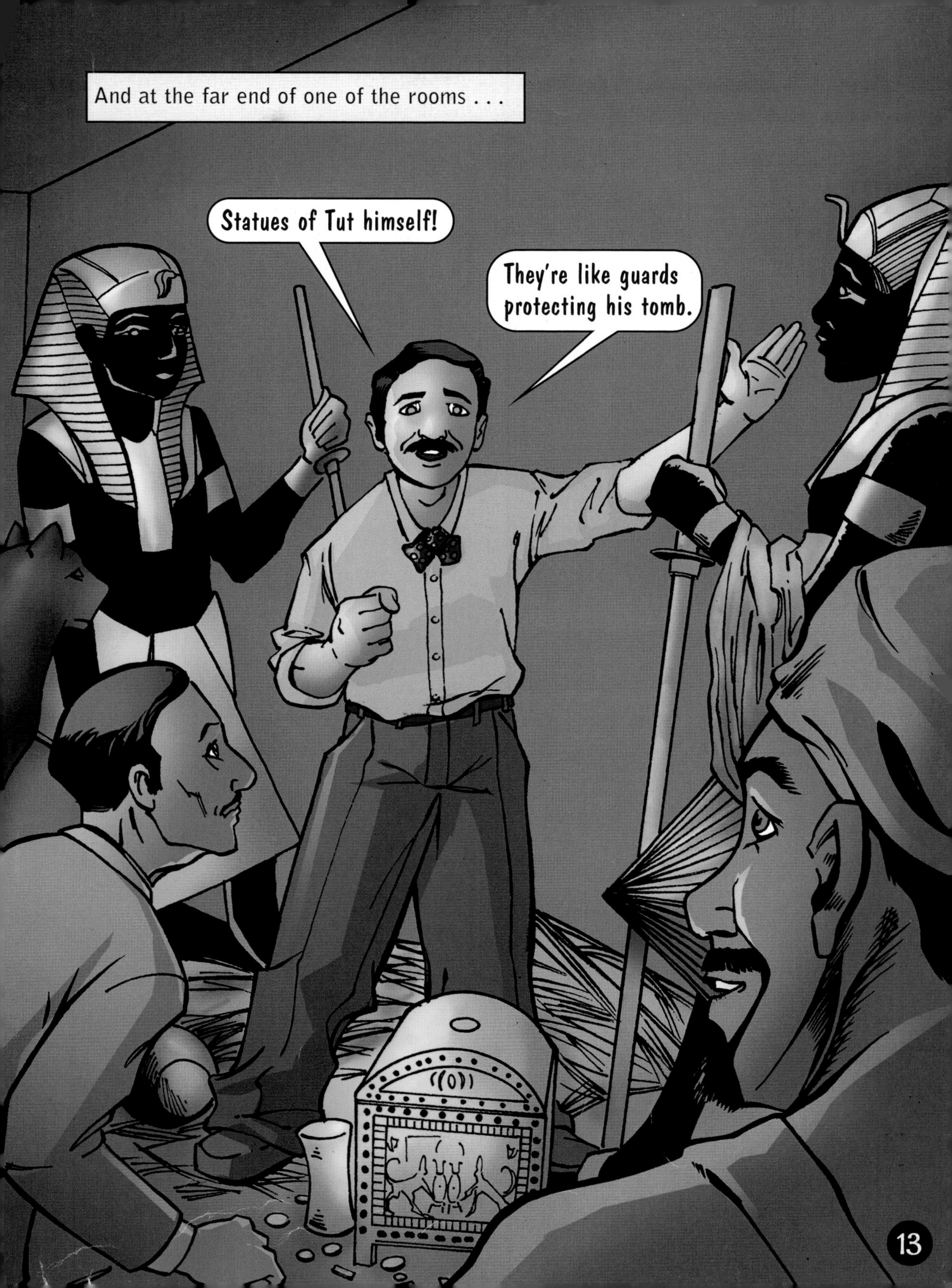
And at the far end of one of the rooms . . .
Statues of Tut himself!
They're like guards protecting his tomb.

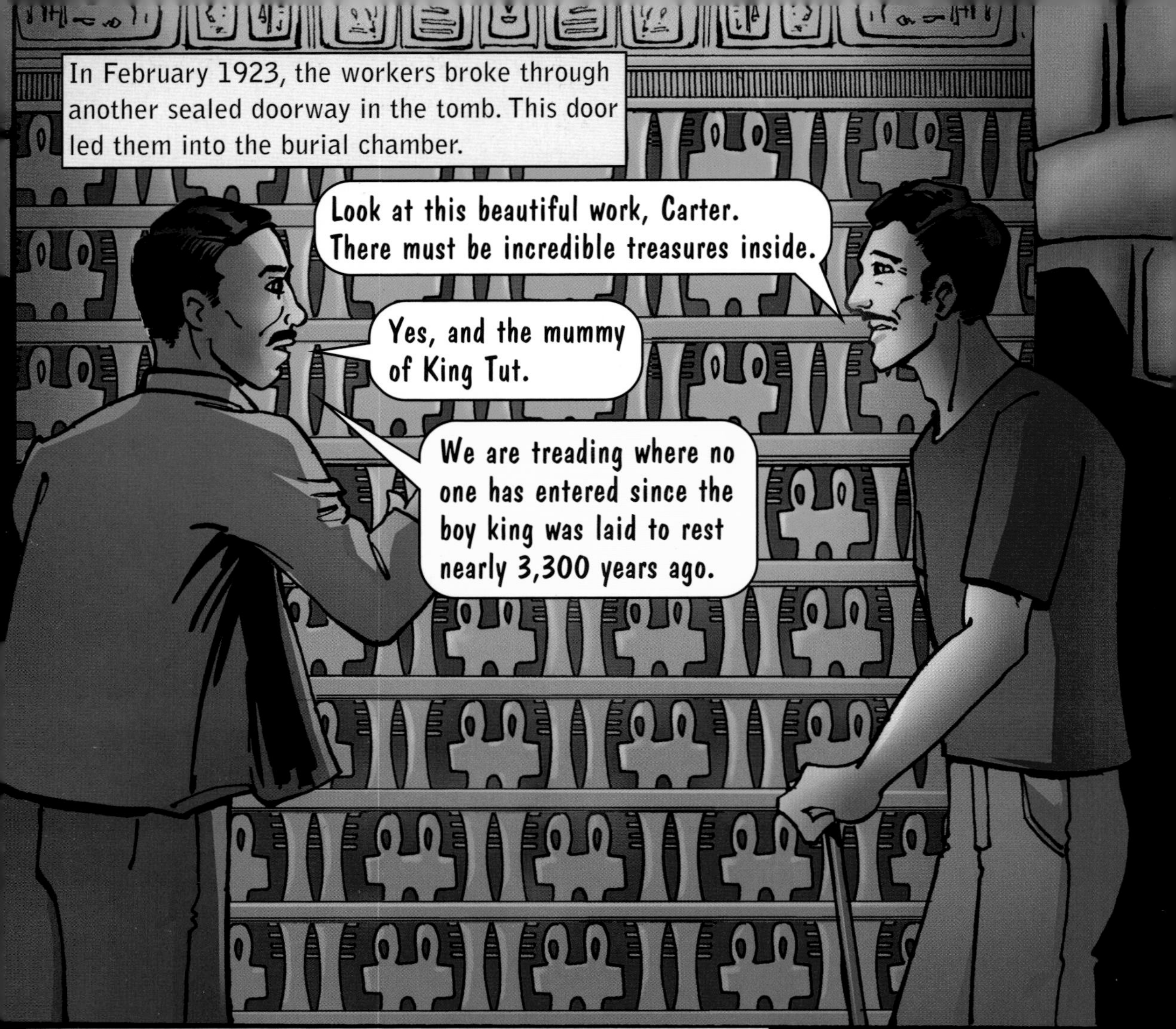
In February 1923, the workers broke through another sealed doorway in the tomb. This door led them into the burial chamber.
Look at this beautiful work, Carter. There must be incredible treasures inside.
Yes, and the mummy of King Tut.
We are treading where no one has entered since the boy king was laid to rest nearly 3,300 years ago.

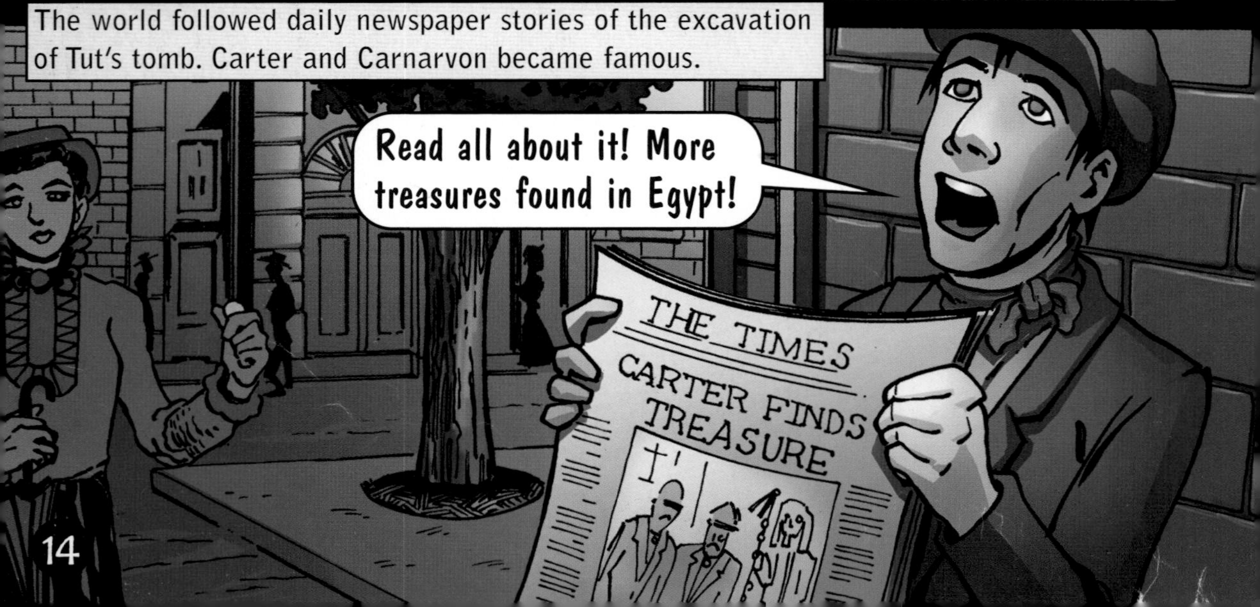
The world followed daily newspaper stories of the excavation of Tut's tomb. Carter and Carnarvon became famous.
Read all about it! More treasures found in Egypt!
THE TIMES
CARTER FINDS TREASURE

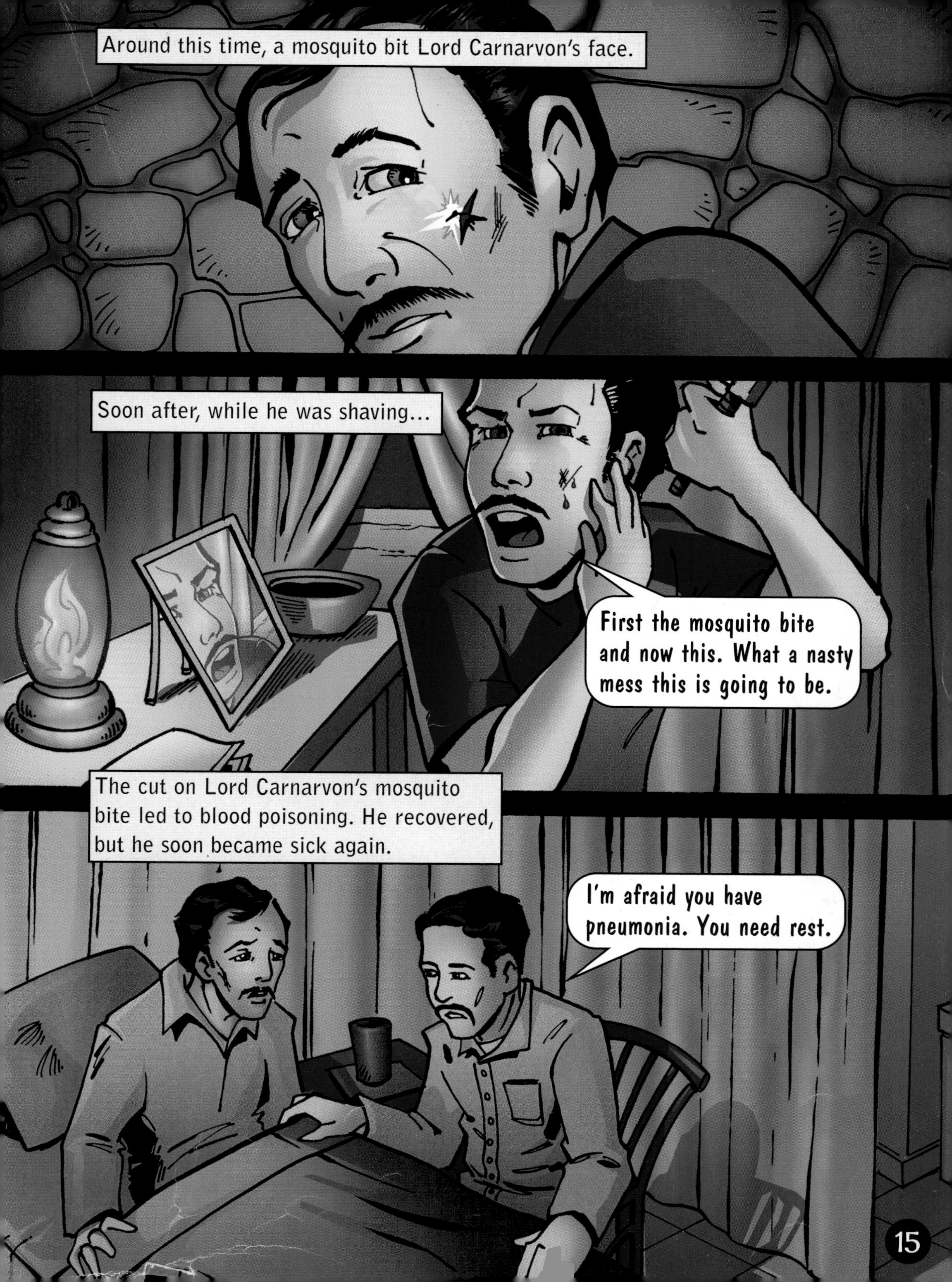

Around this time, a mosquito bit Lord Carnarvon's face.
Soon after, while he was shaving...
First the mosquito bite and now this. What a nasty mess this is going to be.
The cut on Lord Carnarvon's mosquito bite led to blood poisoning. He recovered, but he soon became sick again.
I'm afraid you have pneumonia. You need rest.

CHAPTER 3

THE CURSE AT WORK

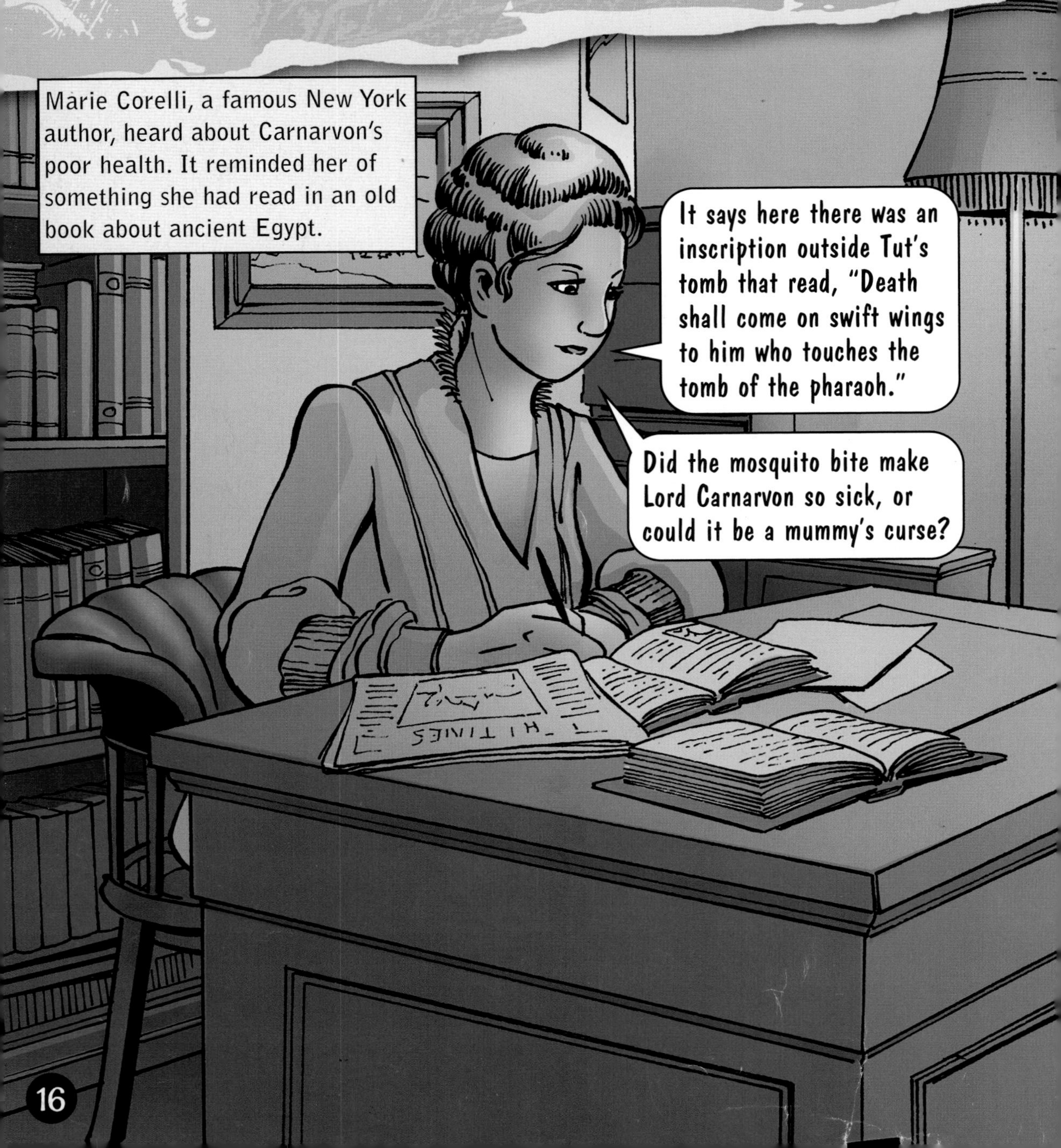

Marie Corelli, a famous New York author, heard about Carnarvon's poor health. It reminded her of something she had read in an old book about ancient Egypt.
It says here there was an inscription outside Tut's tomb that read, "Death shall come on swift wings to him who touches the tomb of the pharaoh."
Did the mosquito bite make Lord Carnarvon so sick, or could it be a mummy's curse?

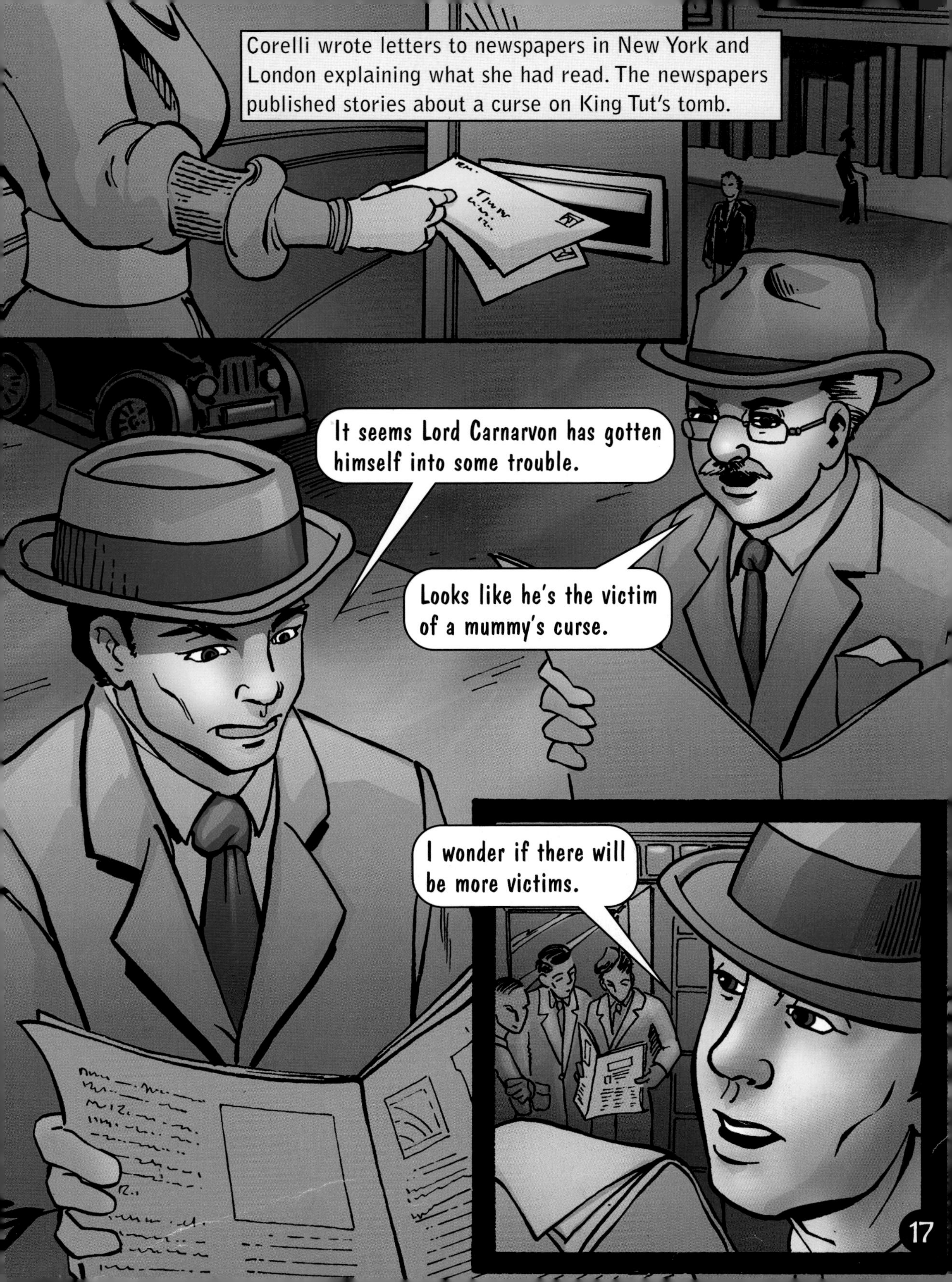
Corelli wrote letters to newspapers in New York and London explaining what she had read. The newspapers published stories about a curse on King Tut's tomb.
It seems Lord Carnarvon has gotten himself into some trouble.
Looks like he's the victim of a mummy's curse.
I wonder if there will be more victims.

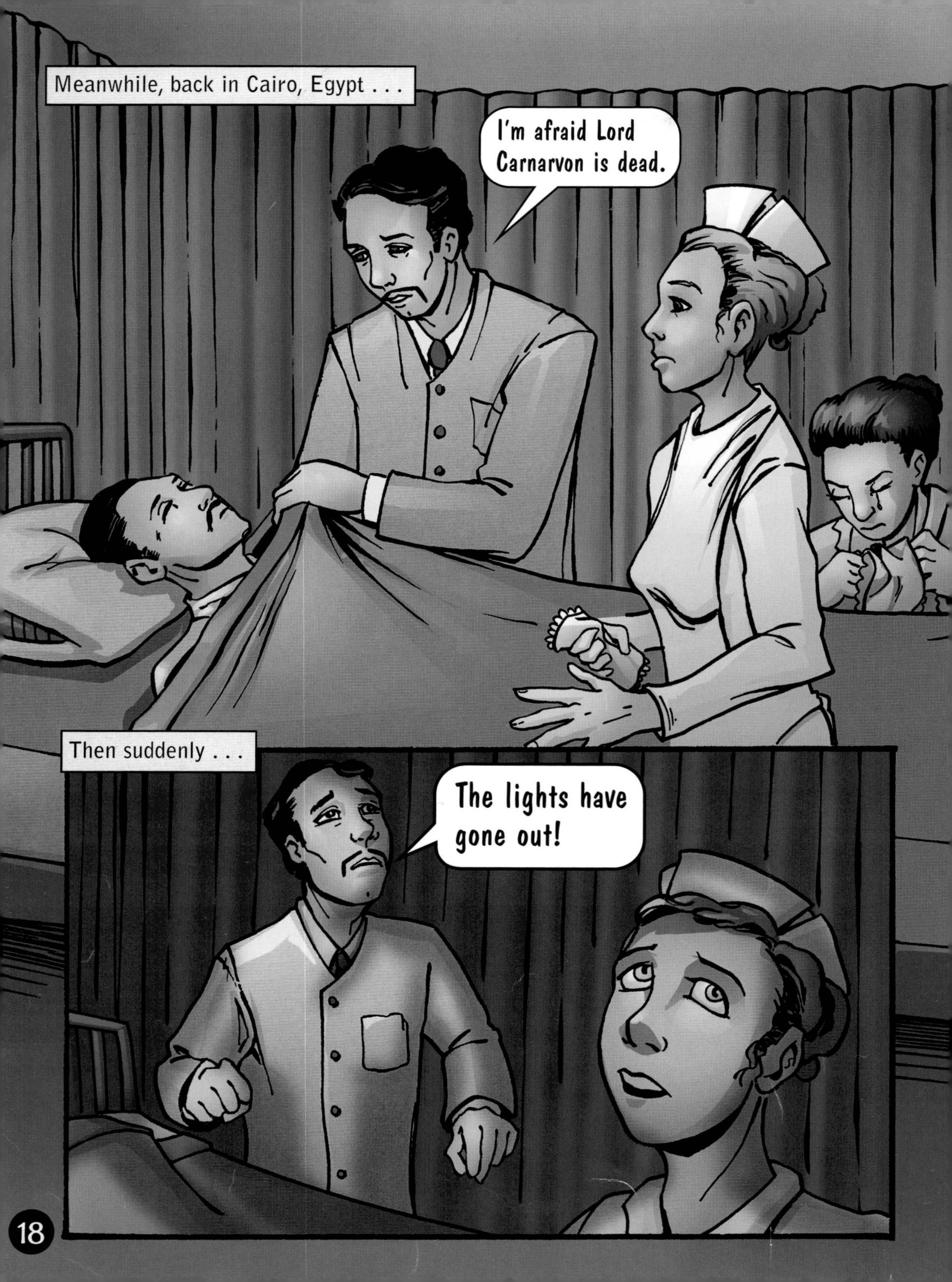
Meanwhile, back in Cairo, Egypt . . .
I'm afraid Lord Carnarvon is dead.
Then suddenly . . .
The lights have gone out!

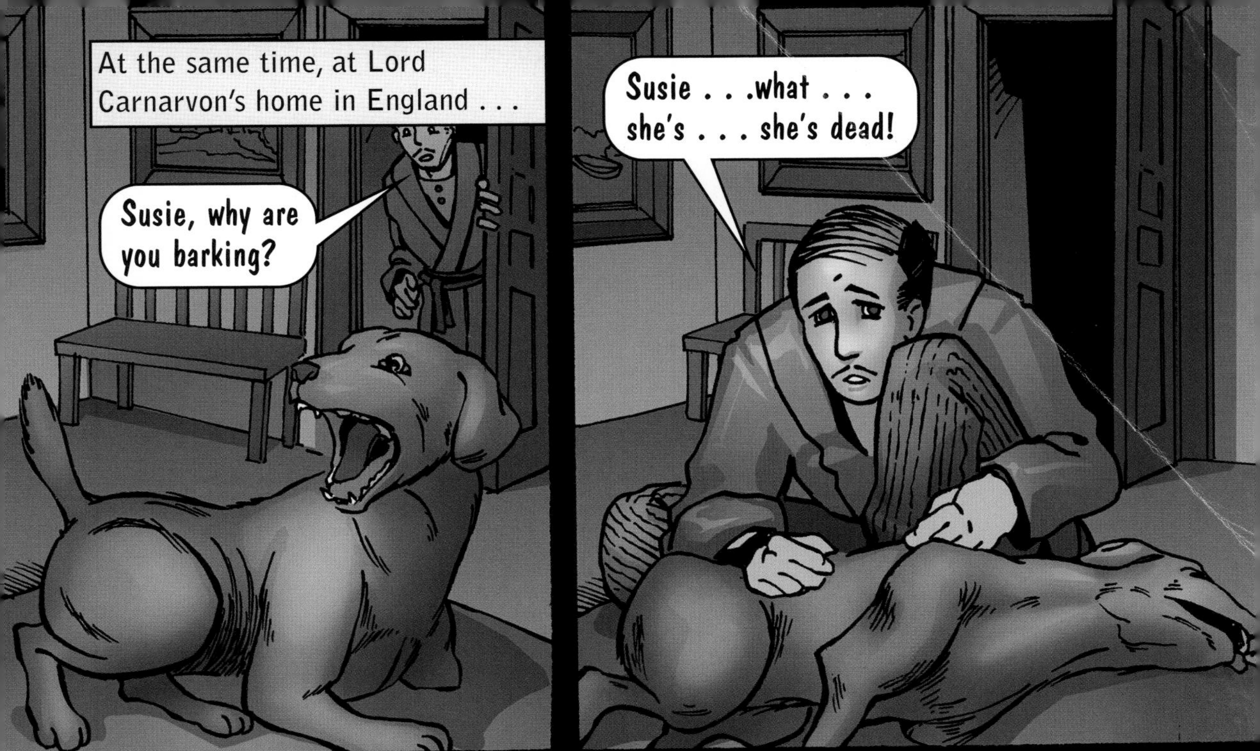
At the same time, at Lord Carnarvon's home in England . . .
Susie, why are you barking?
Susie . . .what . . . she's . . . she's dead!

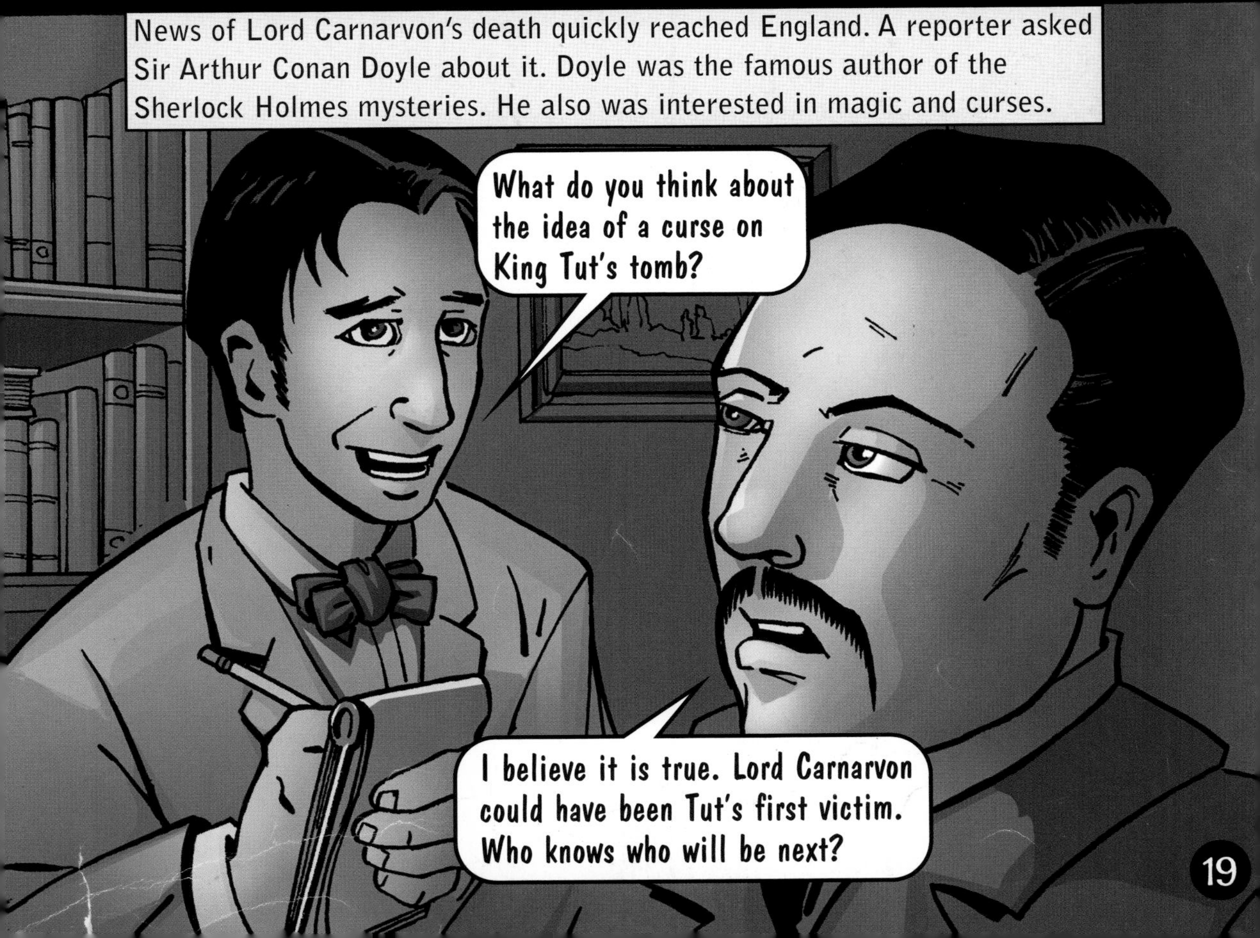
News of Lord Carnarvon's death quickly reached England. A reporter asked Sir Arthur Conan Doyle about it. Doyle was the famous author of the Sherlock Holmes mysteries. He also was interested in magic and curses.
What do you think about the idea of a curse on King Tut's tomb?
I believe it is true. Lord Carnarvon could have been Tut's first victim. Who knows who will be next?

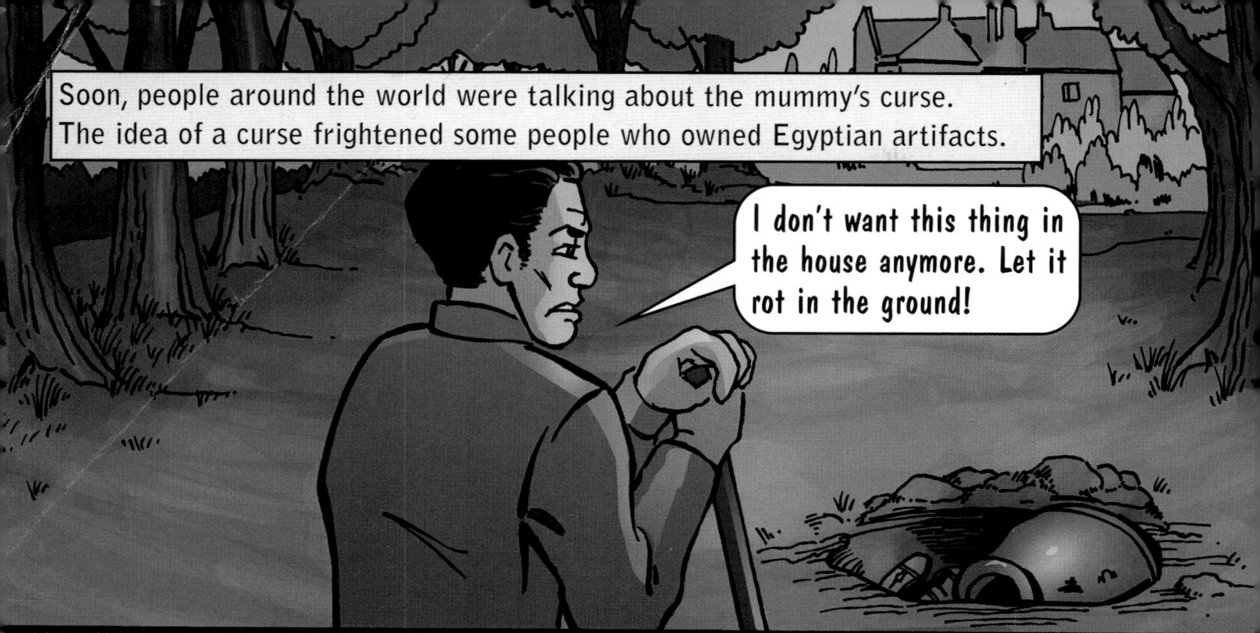
Soon, people around the world were talking about the mummy's curse. The idea of a curse frightened some people who owned Egyptian artifacts.
I don't want this thing in the house anymore. Let it rot in the ground!

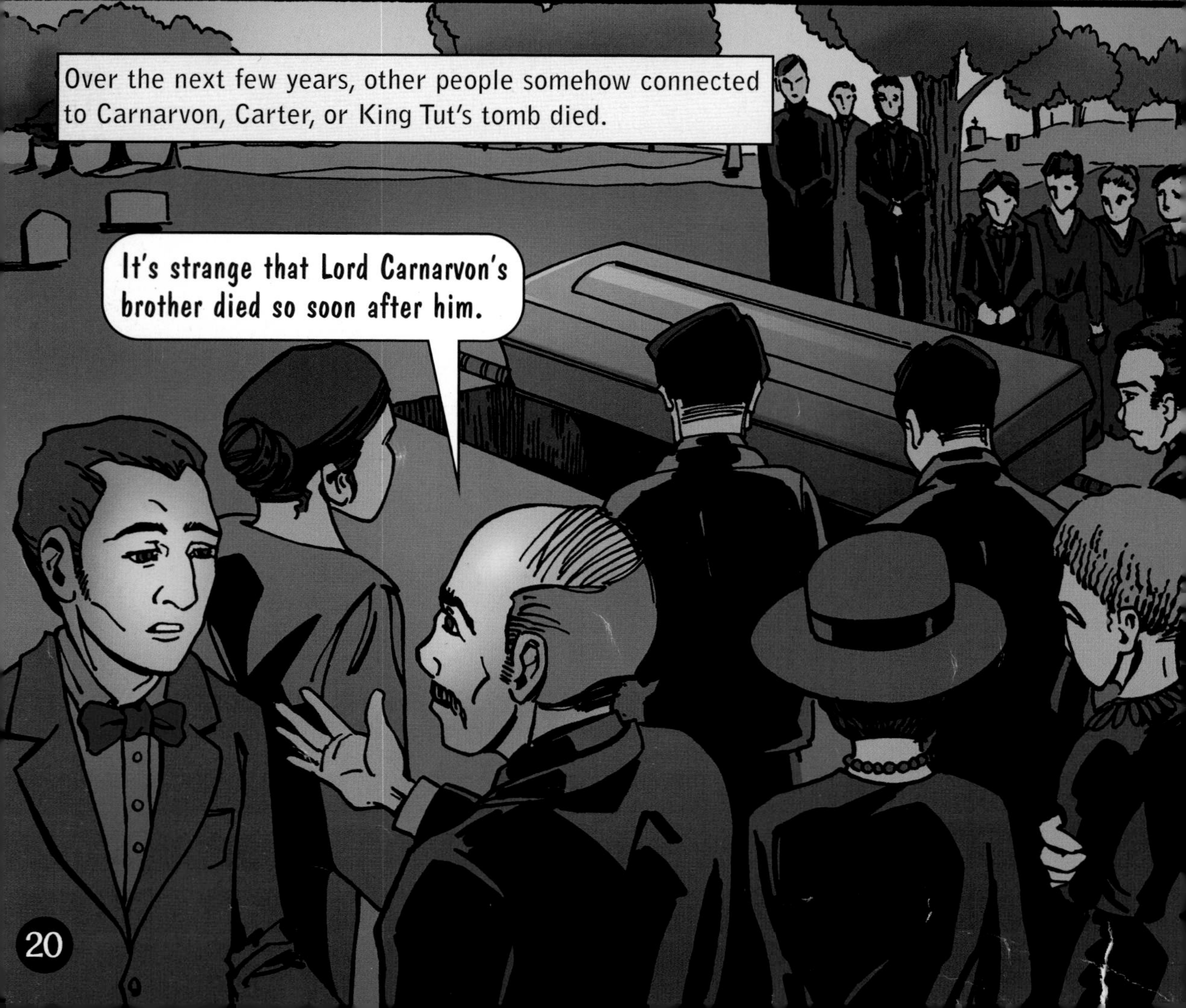
Over the next few years, other people somehow connected to Carnarvon, Carter, or King Tut's tomb died.
It's strange that Lord Carnarvon's brother died so soon after him.

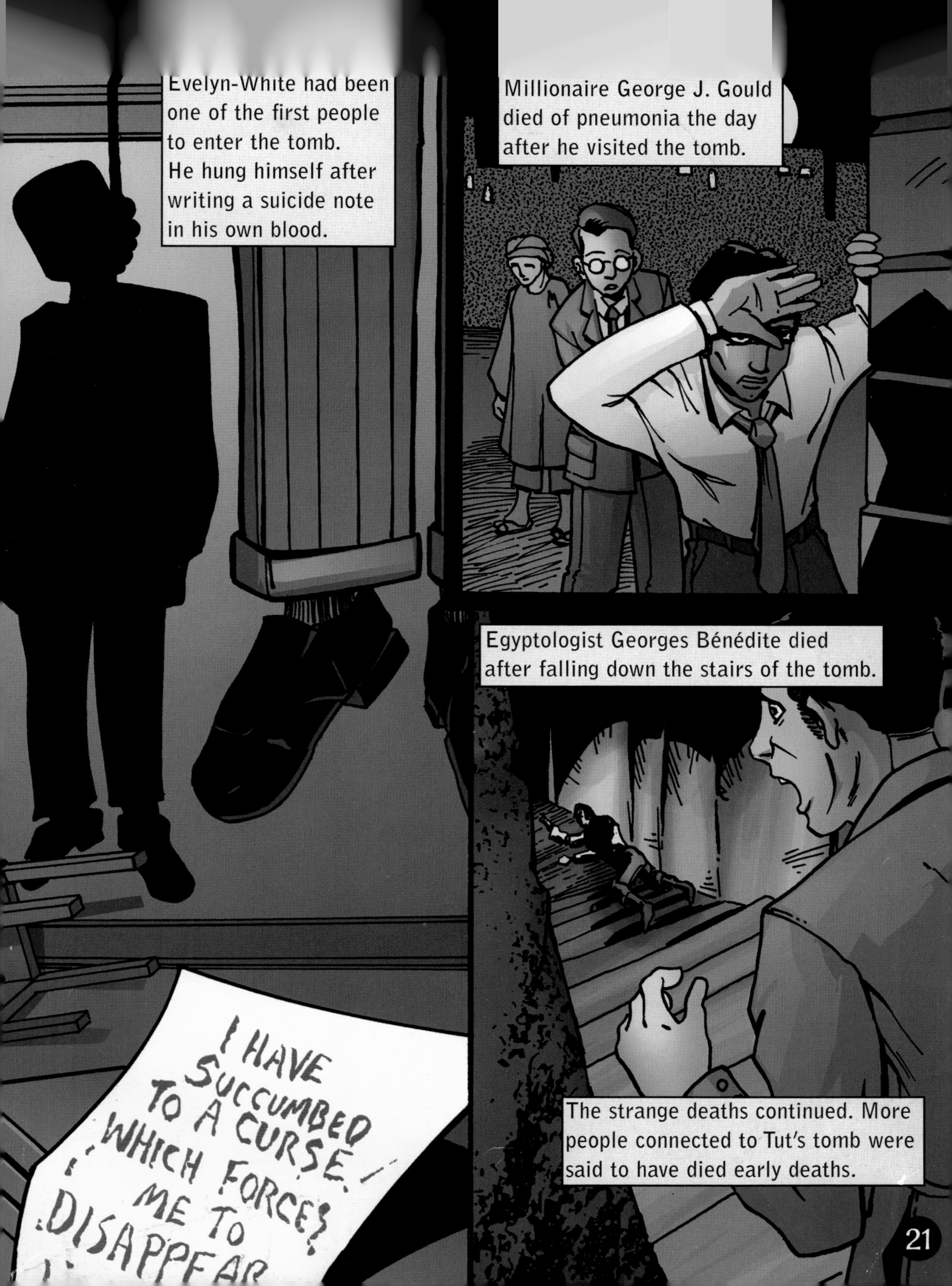
Evelyn-White had been one of the first people to enter the tomb.
He hung himself after writing a suicide note in his own blood.
I HAVE SUCCUMBED TO A CURSE WHICH FORCES ME TO DISAPPEAR
Millionaire George J. Gould died of pneumonia the day after he visited the tomb.
Egyptologist Georges Bénédite died after falling down the stairs of the tomb.
The strange deaths continued. More people connected to Tut's tomb were said to have died early deaths.

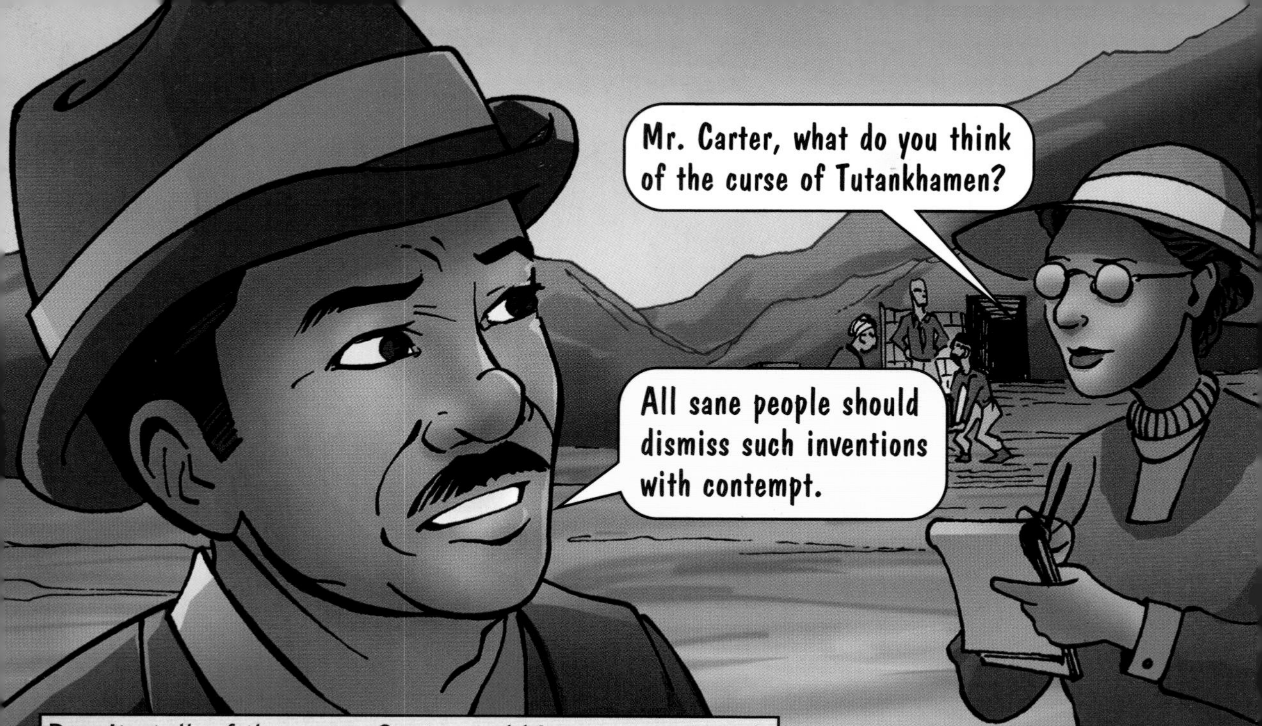
Mr. Carter, what do you think of the curse of Tutankhamen?
All sane people should dismiss such inventions with contempt.

Despite talk of the curse, Carter and his crew continued their difficult work in the tomb. Carter's long-time friend Arthur Callender helped him every step of the way.

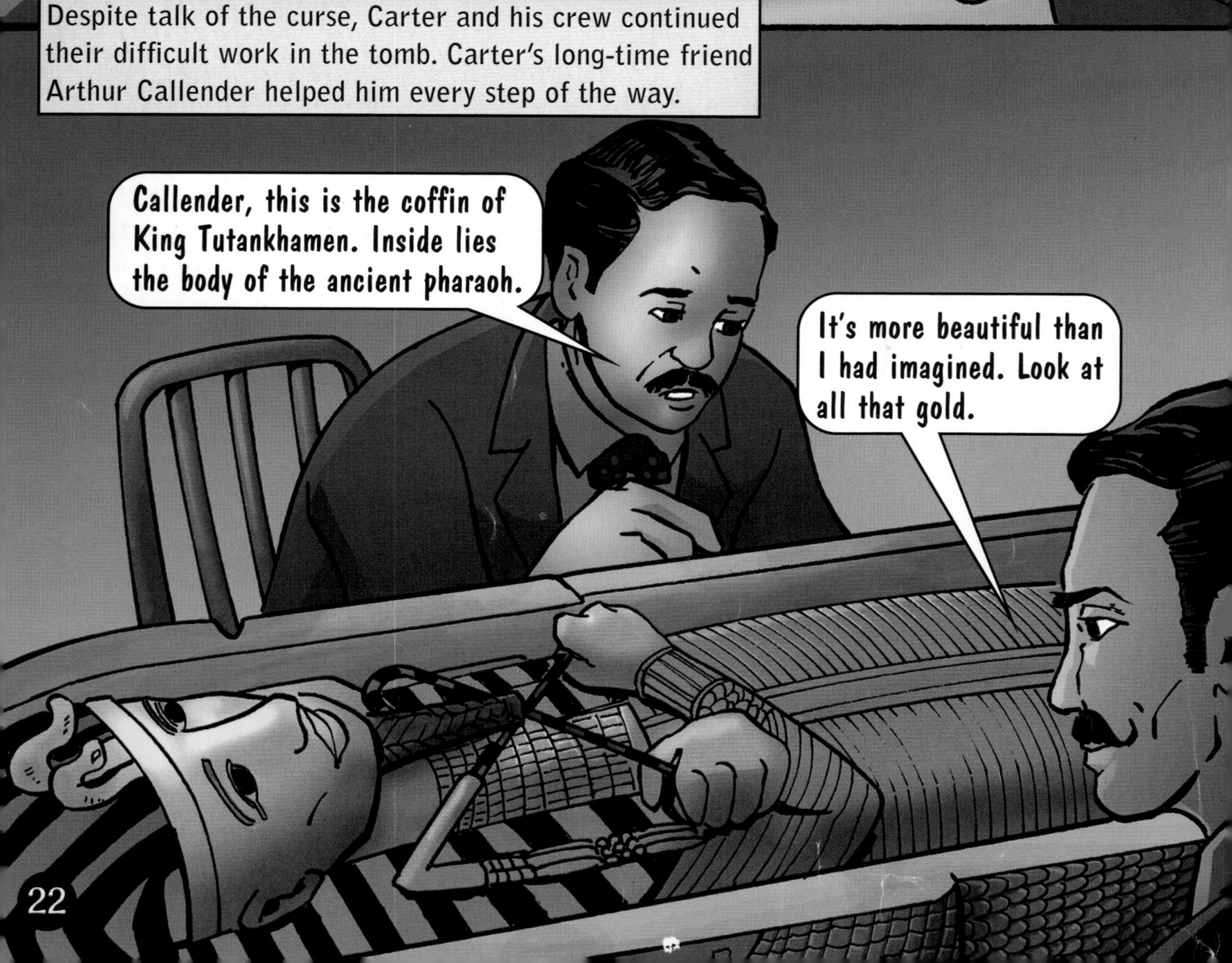
Callender, this is the coffin of King Tutankhamen. Inside lies the body of the ancient pharaoh.
It's more beautiful than I had imagined. Look at all that gold.

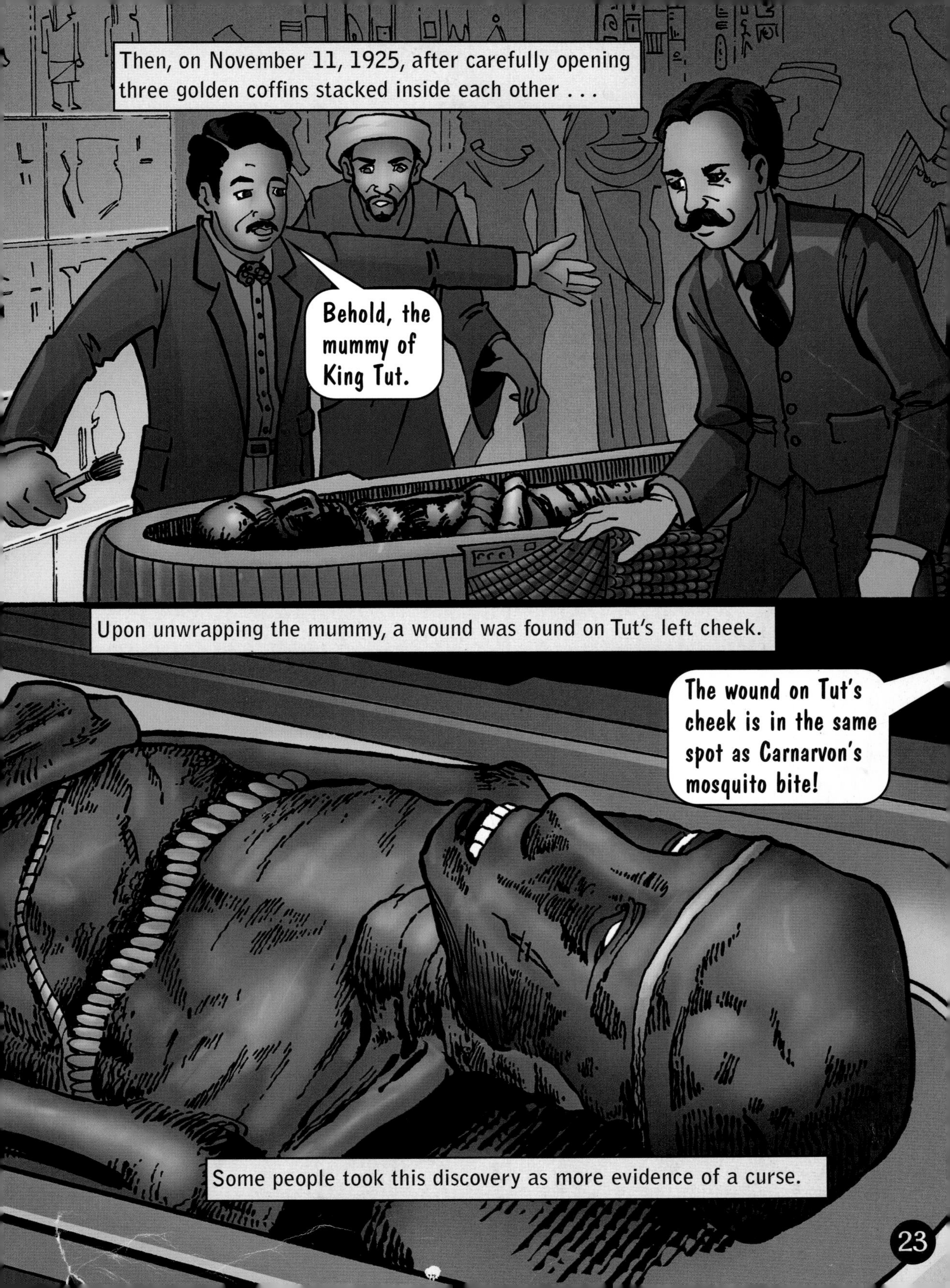
Then, on November 11, 1925, after carefully opening three golden coffins stacked inside each other . . .
Behold, the mummy of King Tut.
Upon unwrapping the mummy, a wound was found on Tut's left cheek.
The wound on Tut's cheek is in the same spot as Carnarvon's mosquito bite!
Some people took this discovery as more evidence of a curse.

Chapter 4

Curse or Myth?

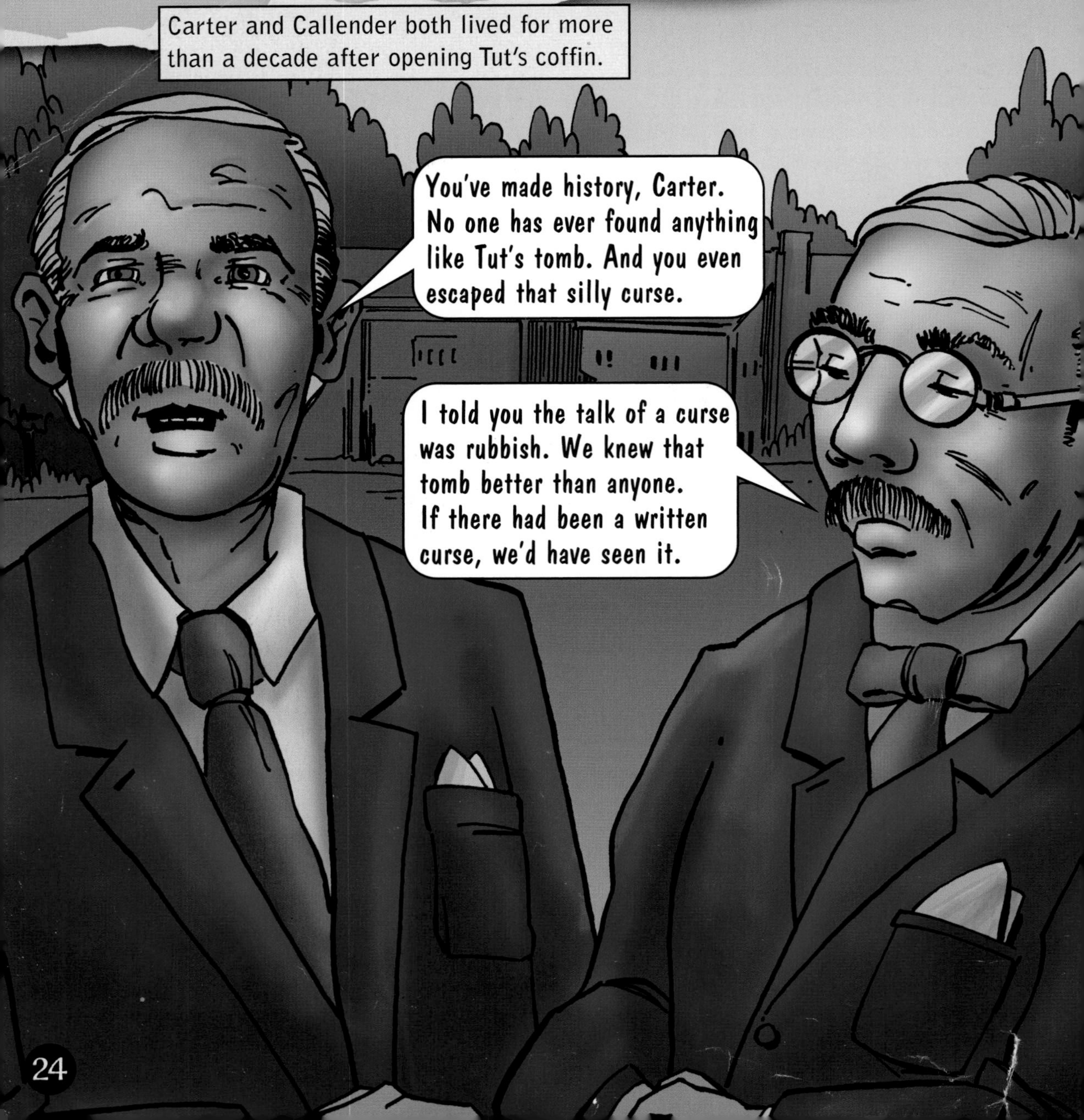

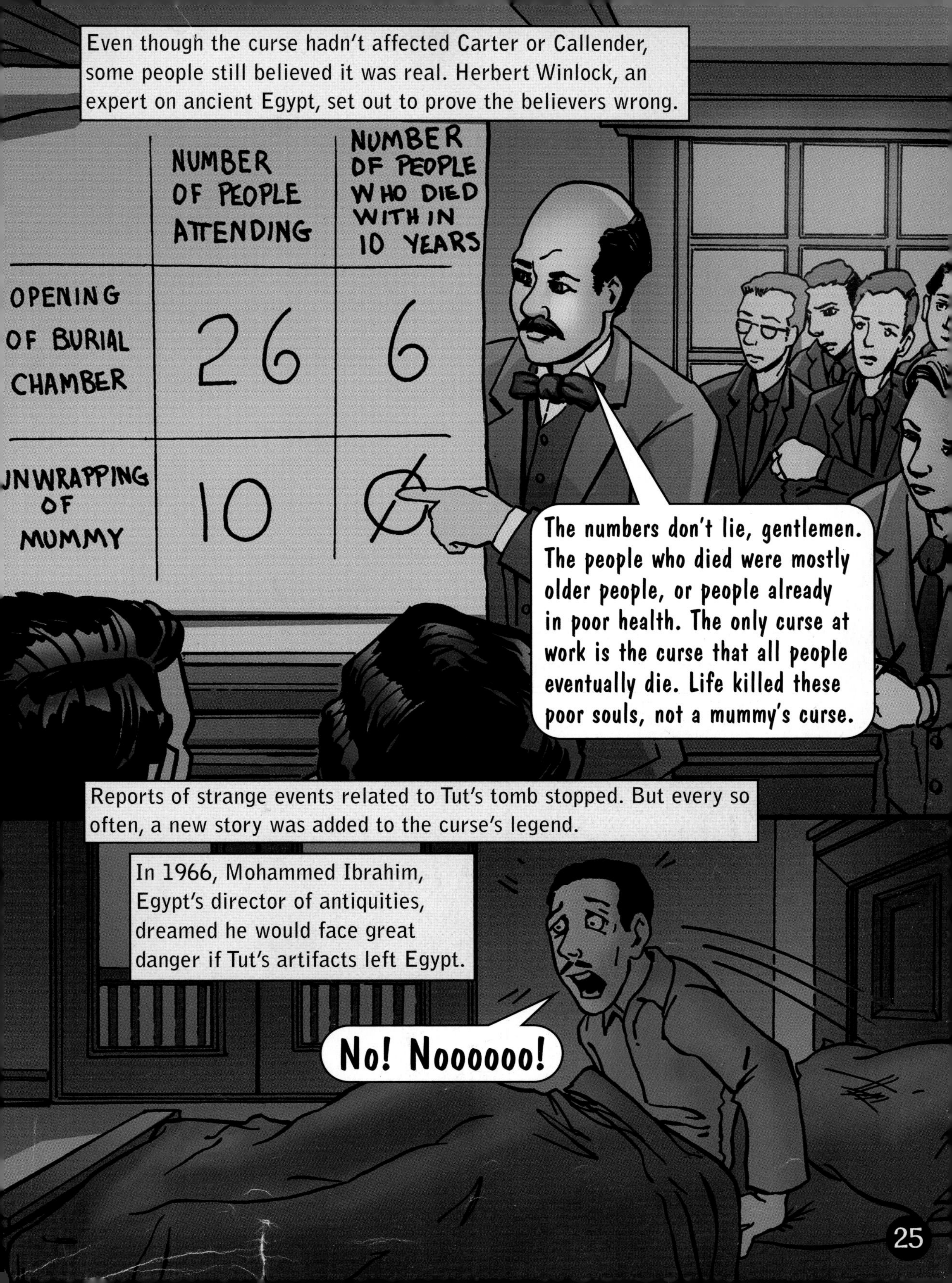
Even though the curse hadn't affected Carter or Callender, some people still believed it was real. Herbert Winlock, an expert on ancient Egypt, set out to prove the believers wrong.
NUMBER OF PEOPLE ATTENDING
NUMBER OF PEOPLE WHO DIED WITHIN 10 YEARS
OPENING OF BURIAL CHAMBER
26
6
UNWRAPPING OF MUMMY
10
0
The numbers don't lie, gentlemen. The people who died were mostly older people, or people already in poor health. The only curse at work is the curse that all people eventually die. Life killed these poor souls, not a mummy's curse.
Reports of strange events related to Tut's tomb stopped. But every so often, a new story was added to the curse's legend.
In 1966, Mohammed Ibrahim, Egypt's director of antiquities, dreamed he would face great danger if Tut's artifacts left Egypt.
No! Noooooo!

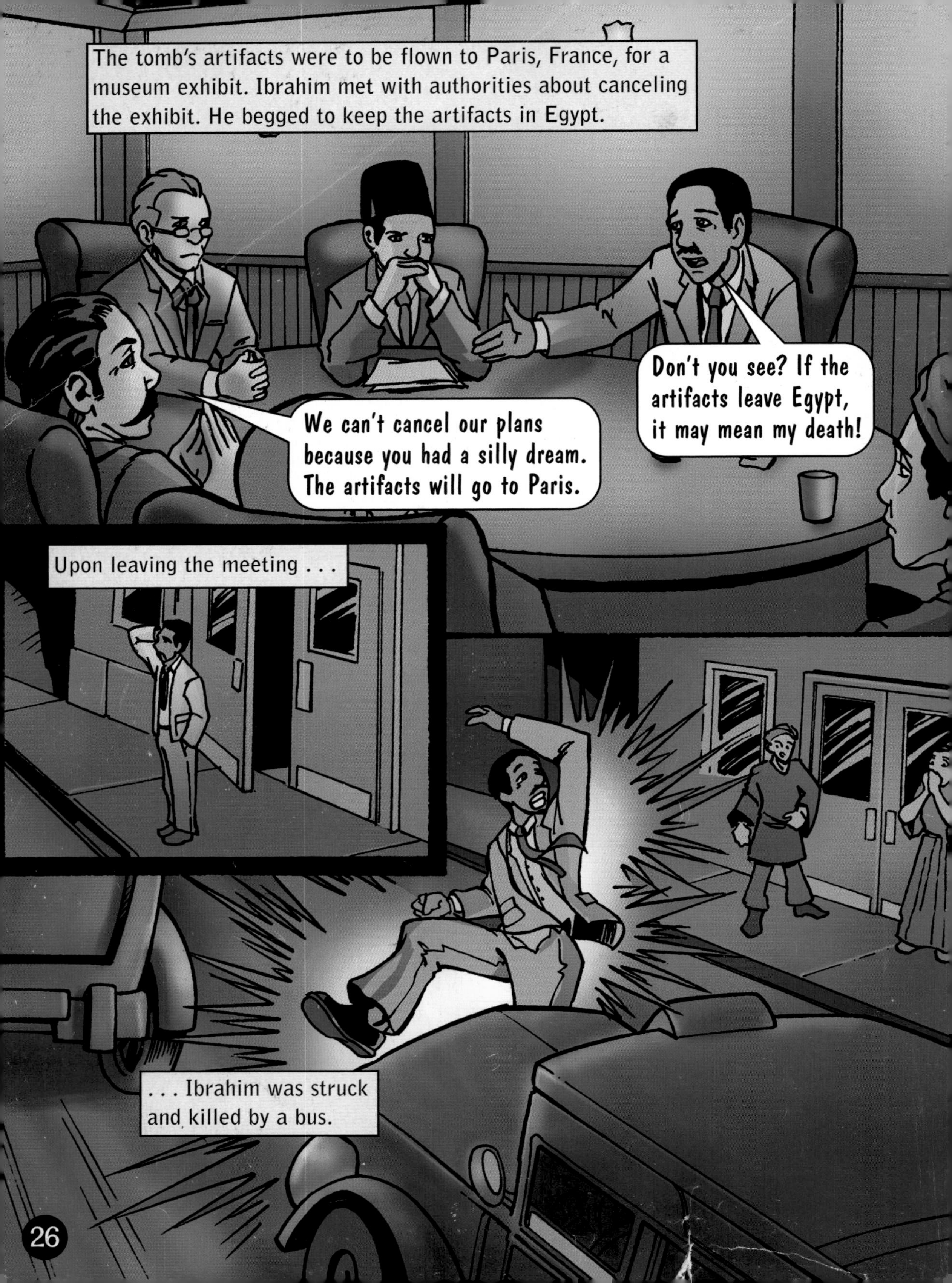
The tomb's artifacts were to be flown to Paris, France, for a museum exhibit. Ibrahim met with authorities about canceling the exhibit. He begged to keep the artifacts in Egypt.
Don't you see? If the artifacts leave Egypt, it may mean my death!
We can't cancel our plans because you had a silly dream. The artifacts will go to Paris.
Upon leaving the meeting . . .
. . . Ibrahim was struck and killed by a bus.

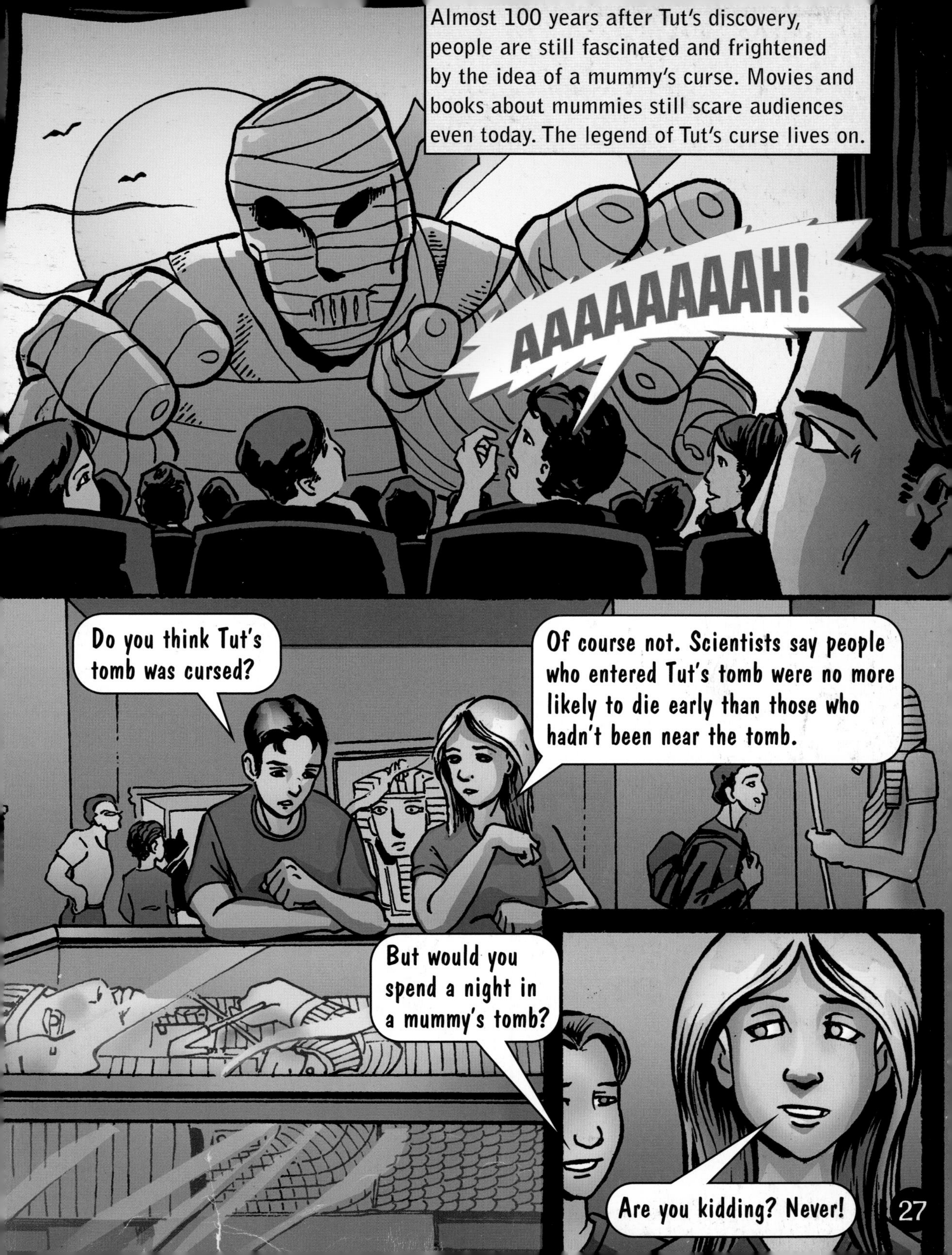
Almost 100 years after Tut's discovery, people are still fascinated and frightened by the idea of a mummy's curse. Movies and books about mummies still scare audiences even today. The legend of Tut's curse lives on.
AAAAAAAAH!
Do you think Tut's tomb was cursed?
Of course not. Scientists say people who entered Tut's tomb were no more likely to die early than those who hadn't been near the tomb.
But would you spend a night in a mummy's tomb?
Are you kidding? Never!

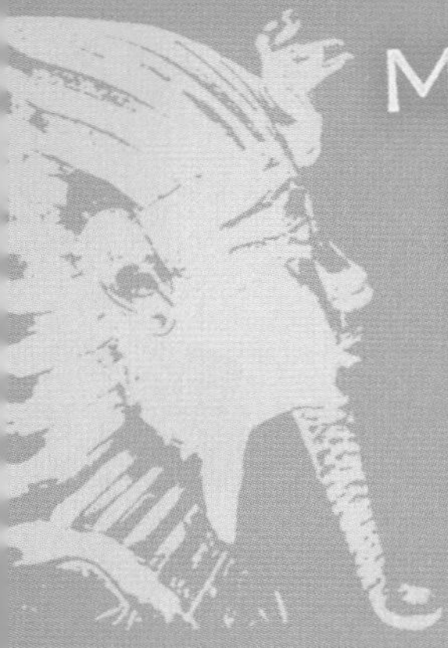

More About King Tut and the Curse

- Many deaths of people connected with King Tut's tomb were odd and mysterious. It's not surprising that these unexplained deaths were mistaken as the result of a curse. One example is the death of Richard Bethell, Howard Carter's personal secretary. Bethell's father, Lord Westbury, killed himself after hearing of his son's death. The car carrying Lord Westbury's body to the cemetery struck and killed an eight-year-old boy.

- King Tut was buried in a tomb meant for someone else. Other ancient Egyptians' names appear on many of the artifacts left in Tut's tomb. Even one of the coffins he is buried in has someone else's name on it.

- Grave robbers probably broke into Tut's tomb shortly after he died. They were caught before much damage was done. Priests reburied the entrance to Tut's tomb, and it stayed buried until Carter found it in 1922.

- Howard Carter was more concerned about getting the treasures from Tut's tomb than in preserving the body. Carter cut Tut's body in three pieces. Today, Tut's body lies in his original burial place. It is carefully protected by the Egyptian government.

Howard Carter found the mummies of two of King Tut's children in the king's tomb. Scientists think both children were female.

Scientists believe that some people who entered Tut's tomb died because of mold or fungus that grew in the tomb. Many kinds of harmful bacteria have been found in Tut's tomb.

Some scientists believe King Tut was murdered. He was only 18 or 19 when he died. X-rays of Tut's skull show that he suffered a blow to the back of his head. He was buried very quickly. The next ruler tried to erase history by removing all records of Tut from official documents.

GLOSSARY

archaeologist (ar-kee-OL-uh-jist)—a scientist who studies the past by looking at old buildings and objects

artifact (AR-tih-fakt)—an object made by humans that was used in the past; tools and weapons are artifacts.

contempt (kuhn-TEMPT)—total lack of respect

excavation (ek-skuh-VAY-shuhn)—a search for ancient remains buried in the ground

exhibit (eg-ZIB-it)—a public display of works of art or historical objects

pneumonia (noo-MOH-nyuh)—a serious disease that makes breathing very difficult

spirit (SPIHR-it)—the part of a person thought to control thoughts and feelings; ancient Egyptians believed the spirit left the body after death and traveled to the afterworld.

INTERNET SITES

FactHound offers a safe, fun way to find Internet sites related to this book. All of the sites on FactHound have been researched by our staff.

Here's how:

1. *Visit www.facthound.com*
2. Type in this special code **0736838333** for age-appropriate sites. Or enter a search word related to this book for a more general search.
3. Click on the **Fetch It** button.

FactHound will fetch the best sites for you!

READ MORE

Burgan, Michael. *King Tut's Tomb: Ancient Treasures Uncovered.* Mummies. Mankato, Minn.: Capstone Press, 2005.

Nardo, Don. *King Tut's Tomb.* Wonders of the World. San Diego: KidHaven Press, 2004.

Pemberton, Delia. *Egyptian Mummies: People From the Past.* San Diego: Harcourt, 2001.

Williams, Brian. *Tutankhamen.* Historical Biographies. Chicago: Heinemann Library, 2002.

BIBLIOGRAPHY

Carter, Howard, and A. C. Mace. *The Tomb of Tut.ankh.Amen, Discovered by the Late Earl of Carnarvon and Howard Carter.* London: Cassell and Company, Ltd., 1923.

El Mahdy, Christine. *Mummies, Myth, and Magic in Ancient Egypt.* New York: Thames and Hudson, 1989.

Entering King Tut's Tomb, 1922. EyeWitness to History. http://eyewitnesstohistory.com/tut.htm.

King, Mike, and Greg Cooper. Discovery Channel: King Tut—Ask the Experts. http://dsc.discovery.com/anthology/unsolvedhistory/kingtut/experts/read.html.

Reeves, Nicholas. *The Complete Tutankhamun: The King, the Tomb, the Royal Treasure.* New York: Thames and Hudson, 1990.

Weintraub, Skye, Dr. Effects of Digestive Disfunction. http://www.femcentre.com/digestive1.pdf.

INDEX